The Findhorn Book of

Guidance & Intuition

by

Carly Newfeld

First published by Findhorn Press 2003

ISBN 1 84409 008 6

British Library Cataloguing-in-Publication Data.
A catalogue record for this book is available from
the British Library.

Edited by Elaine Harrison
Cover and internal book design by Thierry Bogliolo
Cover background photograph by Digital Vision
Cover central photograph ©Thinkstock

Printed and bound by WS Bookwell, Finland

Published by
Findhorn Press
305a The Park, Findhorn
Forres IV36 3TE
Scotland, UK

tel 01309 690582
fax 01309 690036
e-mail: info@findhornpress.com

TABLE OF CONTENTS

INTRODUCTION

One day, while driving to an appointment, I thought about maybe beginning my introduction with the story of how I received guidance to write this book. Almost immediately the internal chatter began, ranging between a dismissive, "No, that's too corny" and an insistent, "Well you did!"

I continued to drive, observing the chatter going on in my head, ignoring much of it, but noticing one insistent voice. It wasn't a particularly loud voice; neither was it a "still, small voice," rather it had a ring to it that I recognised as my authentic voice. Whenever I hear it I pay attention. I shifted in my seat and sat taller. It was the voice that had earlier said: "Well, you did!" Clear and unfettered by emotion, commanding but not demanding, it even had a slightly humorous tone to it. The other voices simply faded into the background.

My inner voice is very clear to me, though it has taken practice to distinguish it amid the clamour within and without. The aim of this book is to help you to learn how to recognise your own inner voice when you hear it, to understand the subtle ways it speaks to you, and to gather the energy, inspiration and courage to follow its lead.

So, yes I did receive guidance to write this book. Though on this occasion it was a quiet guidance, a feeling rather than words. It all started with an e-mail from Findhorn Press about a new series of books they were planning to publish; the e-mail included a list of subjects for the intended books and they looked intriguing. Among the long and varied list was Finding Your Guidance.

I read through the list several times, and though the topics were varied and fascinating, my eyes kept stopping on the word Guidance. I didn't intend to stop there – at least not consciously – yet I did. Every time I read it, I felt a sense of expansiveness, clarity and assuredness. There was no voice; in fact there was none of the usual internal dialogue. Instead, I felt unusually quiet inside. I didn't see a raven swoop past my window or a flash of light, I didn't hear a fanfare and neither did the phone ring at that exact moment to confirm my decision. I just knew. Something deep down within me relaxed as if I'd just completed a series of prana yoga breaths. My confirmation came simply from my mind and body feeling in harmony and at rest. That was the book I had to write.

Having lived in the Findhorn Community in the very early days (1970 to 1978), I had the privilege of working closely with two of the founders, Dorothy Maclean and Eileen Caddy, observing first hand the quiet magnificence of spiritual guidance in their lives, and how they followed their guidance implicitly. Never did I imagine then that I would be writing about it and helping others to find their own guidance.

My first year at Findhorn was spent in the Foundation's office, where my morning routine included typing up Eileen's daily guidance and delivering it to our community printer, Victor Bailey, by 9.30am. Each and every morning, on her way out of the Sanctuary, Eileen would pass me her little notebook of handwritten guidance; putting on my glasses to help me decipher her tiny, unique handwriting, I would then carefully transcribe her words, verbatim, onto special paper ready for printing. There was little time to spare. The printed version had to be distributed no later than 10.00am, in time for community members to read over tea and biscuits.

Dorothy also shared her own special guidance received from the

Landscape Angel and the Devas with the garden group. At 10.30 each morning she and I would take a break from our office work and head over to her cosy caravan for a milky coffee – a primitive version of latte. Over coffee I would learn about the loving nature of guidance and the joyfulness that accompanies communication and co-operation with the Devic realm. Probably one of the most important lessons was that a pre-requisite to receiving guidance was an impeccable attunement with one's own wholeness. Like Eileen, Dorothy's daily discipline of inner listening and meditation instilled in her an effortless way to recognise, hear and follow direction from the God within.

In 1971, Eileen received a very specific piece of guidance advising that she was no longer to receive guidance for the community as a whole; that the next step in our communal spiritual practice was to learn how to turn within and receive guidance for ourselves. I Bless Eileen – and God – for that, for it was indeed a turning point in my own life and a step towards writing this book.

The Findhorn Book of Guidance & Intuition explores the many ways in which we can access spiritual guidance, heed intuition, and follow what we receive with diligence and joy. The stories I present here define the steps taken by people whose clear guidance and intuition is as integral to their daily lives as brushing their teeth.

In particular, there are chapters dedicated to the founders of the Findhorn Community, Eileen and Peter Caddy and Dorothy Maclean, whose faith and guidance formed the foundation upon which the community was built. The three represented a trinity of Love, Light and Wisdom, qualities that for me became the touchstone for my own wholeness and inner listening. Thanks to them I am able to recognise the presence and voice of God amid the often-busy internal chatter. Whenever I wonder about my own guidance I ask inwardly: "Does it bring and reveal love? Does it bear the truth of light? And does it carry the clarity of wisdom?"

My intent is that the words in this book will confirm, clarify, inform and inspire. A primer for those of you wondering about spiritual guidance in the traditional sense of the word, and a reminder for those well along a path of exploring consciousness who may need an encouraging hand. At the end of this book you will find a bibliography and list of recommended books and web sites that may speak to your particular way of receiving guidance and following intuition. Thank you in advance to all of you who read these words. Your intent to live as closely as you can from the inside will lead you and, as you go about your day, your gentle, inner authority will enliven and inspire others. Being ourselves is all we really ever need to do.

Enjoy,

Carly Newfeld

Santa Fe, New Mexico

Overview

The Spirit of Guidance

"Don't learn it with your head, but with your heart, your intuition."
[Hilda Charlton]

Researching this book required me to speak with numerous people, and I began to see a thread I had long suspected but – until now – had never confirmed. The thread is that there is a common feeling or "tone" associated with the moment of clarity each person referred to as "guidance" or an "intuitive flash." Musician, Mike calls it "a go feeling." Bernadette, a potter from one of Northern New Mexico's Indian pueblos, told me how everything just "lined up" for her. An acupuncturist friend, Sally, said that "everything would just fall into place" and that she could "see the connection between things."

Sally's awareness of the body's meridian system as a microcosm of the wholeness of creation, helped her to understand how, in fact, things really *do* fall into place; and how alignment allows us to access information and knowledge, which might otherwise be hidden from view. Whether we choose to call that knowledge "guidance," or the information "intuition" doesn't really matter, both are ways to define the tone that feels or sounds different from the usual background chatter. A tone that emanates from the source of life itself, the source of vitality, prana, breath, and Spirit, which connects us all in the unified field of consciousness.

One day, many years ago, while meditating on the meaning of "The Word" – in the Biblical sense – I realised that "in the beginning" The Word was my own first breath. Throughout that morning I decided to practise letting The Word breathe itself. At first, as I completed my meditation, I sighed a deep imperceptible "Aaahh." I repeated it several times with my eyes closed and observed my breath become even and steady. I went about my day quietly, remembering from time to time to notice my breathing. Suddenly – while contemplating a problem – in a flash of inner illumination came the breath of "Ah ha!" A wonderful, uplifting, opening "Ah ha" moment, when with a quickening of breath the mist cleared before my eyes, and a rush of energy coursed through my body as new information literally appeared before my inner vision. That particular "Ah ha" moment was lightning fast; at other times my "Ah ha's" come slowly, with gentleness and a deep relaxing of my body, mind and spirit, followed by an enhanced ability to think and perceive in an imperceptibly altered state of reality.

How do we reach this source – or how does it reach us? As I write this, I do not visualise one fixed point as the source, but an ever-turning series of wheels within wheels, like the cosmos itself, the arch of the night sky or the Circle of the Directions – sacred to indigenous peoples of the world. Each human soul, each individual consciousness has the ability to be in alignment with that ever-changing, fluid wheel. At the moment of alignment – which can happen ten times a day, hardly ever at all, or almost continually – we have an opportunity to seek or receive guidance. In fact, I will go so far as to say it is always available to us and what we call "synchronicity" is a confirmation of being aligned and attuned, of being in the flow of life. We only "miss" when we are busy in our minds, ahead of ourselves, worrying about the future or living in the past. My friend, Bruce, refers to this as "the trance," he believes we're in the trance any time we are not being simply and effortlessly present.

But why does it matter whether we are aligned or not? Does it matter whether we make our decisions based on guidance or on the advice of others, reason or experience, rational or practical calculated thought? Why guidance?

Why intuition? And what about good, old-fashioned common sense and decisions based on long-held traditional values? This book may raise as many questions as it answers, and that's not a bad thing. It is essential we each find our own way through; we each find our own, unique voice that we learn to trust implicitly.

Receiving guidance does not exclude common sense, and perhaps as a disclaimer I should say right up front, that if you wake up one morning with a voice in your head that tells you to do something that could harm another then don't! It is very unlikely that such a voice came from a benevolent source of life, from God. If your guidance instructs you to harm yourself or another, ignore it and seek help. Pick up the phone and call a trusted friend or family member, a crisis line, or someone from your circle of faith.

There are several vital points I want to make before detailing the different forms guidance may take. *Receiving guidance is not a spiritual privilege: it is available to all.* My personal belief is that finding one's own voice is more than essential – it is urgent. Why? Because learning how to listen deeply, to access guidance, to recognise intuition, and to summon the courage and discipline required to follow it all the way through, is a skill that will certainly be life changing, and possibly even life saving. If each of us can find and listen to our authentic voice – our life-line to the source of life itself – then we may find ourselves a place of safety in the midst of a crisis; we may, step-by-step, find the optimal way we can be of real service to others; we may find a quiet sanctuary inside ourselves in the midst of a storm of protests.

It may not even be our own life we save – it might be the life of another. And if not a human life, it may be a way of life we can save. In fact, our known and familiar way of life is threatened. Depending on where you live at this moment and your choice of lifestyle and friends, it may not appear very threatened, but look around. Look beyond even the environmental destruction of our ecosystems, beyond poverty and homelessness, health crises, child abuse, addiction, racism, violence and war; beyond is a silent, almost invisible force: the slow elimination of our own freedom of thought.

Very little that we read in the newspapers, see on television, or find on the popular news-related web sites is the uncensored truth. Most everything we read or view in the media is carefully edited – or essential information is excluded. Here in the United States huge corporations own radio stations, and publishing conglomerates control the distribution of educational material to schools and books for public libraries and national-chain bookstores. Advertising is becoming ever more slick and subtle as moguls realise the power we have to mute TV ads with the touch of a clicker. Many commercial interruptions have been replaced by "product placement," showing our favourite characters drinking our favourite brand of pop. When we suddenly wake up and realise why that is our favourite brand, we break a chink in the matrix which overlays our modern life. Imagine being able to widen the chink in the matrix, to forge our own personal path through, or even break down the wall altogether.

Access to our own inner, spiritual and practical guidance, a hot line to intuition, a clear and prayerful path, are all ways – perhaps even the most efficient ways – to ensure our minds remain relatively undisturbed by the torrent of information, advice, commands and instructions that surround us. We are not immune to any of this external influence, indeed we may even enjoy and desire it, but it is important to remember that *it* is not *us*. The skill required to navigate through the media storms of the information age is one worth learning and mastering. Though this may require dedication and practise, once learned, nothing can shake true guidance. Our access to pure life force, to our own internal power and our private, intuitive, unlimited line of credit with God, with Spirit, provides the only true protection and sustenance during the storm.

If you think this sounds impossible, realise that every indigenous culture in the world has a name for guidance and intuition, and in some cases not a name so much as a way of being in their world, so integrated is it into their daily life that it has no need for a name. When you access your inner guidance, you join millions and millions of people down the ages who live from inside themselves, knowing that is where true guidance of Spirit originates. Looking around me, I believe this access is ancient, primal and probably integral to our survival as a species.

Many of us have come so far away from this interior place we now need books and workshops to show us the way back, to nudge us in the direction of our innate authenticity and ability to listen to the directive from our soul. Though you cannot fast-track and learn how to access your guidance in a weekend workshop, you can take the first steps back inside and make a decision to go forward, step-by-step, practising, listening and quietening outer voices. As we journey back inside ourselves the outer voices fade into the background and have less claim on our consciousness. We see them for what they are.

Forging our personal path takes many forms, and even the language of guidance differs. In Chapter Two, I tell Eileen Caddy's story of her earliest days hearing the "still, small voice" of God within. While that expression has been used for centuries to denote the voice arising from the peace inside the human heart, "which passeth all understanding," others tell me that their guidance comes not from a still, small voice, but from the LOUDEST voice!

My friend, Joseph, tells me the voice he recognises as his guidance is the one "making all the racket." He explains how it has shown him the right path again and again, though he sometimes hasn't paid attention until it got *really* loud:

> For me, the 'small voice' was the one that whispered in my ear all the things I was 'supposed' to do. One time, when I *knew* I should change jobs, all I could hear was the fear-filled, nagging, small voice inside that went on about the bills, mortgage, car payment, insurance . . . and on and on. I think of it as the small voice because if I listen to it I contract. Its intention is to keep me small inside, to prevent me from taking risks and evolving – from getting bigger.
>
> The 'loud voice' was reminding me in ways I couldn't deny; and when I ignored that voice, I became ill or had odd accidents. And *still* the small whiny, fear-filled voice tried to talk me out of changing jobs! Only then did I recognise the difference. The whiney voice was very, very scared. It was the voice of fear. Fear about loss of security and how I'd manage to pay the mortgage, etc. It had a life of its own which I think I had reinforced by listening to and believing in all the expectations of everyone

around me – including my own!

Perhaps it was just me, but I needed a BIG voice, one that said, 'STOP – that's enough.' If I hadn't finally gotten the message, I bet God would have organised for a plane to fly over my house trailing a bright red and yellow banner with the words 'JOE, LISTEN!' emblazoned upon it.

When we take those first tentative steps into our interior selves, we step into what my dear friend Bruce calls the real world:

Being real enlivens, teaches and leads us, and it originates from the individual soul and spirit. It is grounded, respectful, earthy, often confusing, sometimes stupid, and sometimes brilliant. It brings you home to your body. When you begin to live from a real place you cannot go back even if you want to. You expand your beliefs and attitudes beyond where you think you can. This enables you to see through not only your own eyes, but also through those of your perceived enemy, as well as the eyes of those close to you.

Being real requires a willingness – and willingness is the key word – to live life without blame, anger or judgment.

Bruce continued as if he could hear my unspoken questions:

If you decide that you are willing to live without blaming this doesn't mean you're free of that reaction, only that you can observe yourself blaming or judging and have the option to change your own action; no matter what the other person does. And don't waste energy on judging yourself either – keep moving.

"Intending to become your own authority – believing your own perceptions before the opinions of others – requires an inner discipline that may feel impossible at times. Use the doubt and fear as stepping-stones instead of obstacles. When you step out of the learned programme, every action originates from within you. You will begin to notice that the daily actions of being real are too freeing, too energising and alive to return to the cultural trance, busyness, and worry.

Tears of recognition surfaced as I listened to his words. He concluded:

And, Carly, more than anything, being real requires softening your heart – and sometimes that's the scariest bit of all.

PART ONE

THE FOUNDATIONS OF GUIDANCE & INTUITION

Chapter 1

INTUITION, INSTINCT, INTENT AND IMAGINATION

"The mind is the last to know things!"

[Author unknown]

I sat with Allison drinking iced fruity tea in her lovely garden. Carrying my raspberry tea spritzer, I had chosen a wooden bench under a shady apricot tree, while Allison curled up on a bright yellow deckchair nearby. Looking around me at the vibrant flowers, I wondered how she managed to keep every plant alive and flourishing in the midst of the most severe high desert drought in over fifty years.

"I was guided all the way," she told me. "Guided to plant a garden using drought-tolerant shrubs and flowers, to choose this neighbourhood, to buy this house, even guided to Santa Fe from the East Coast."

"How?" I asked. "Do you hear a voice, consult an astrologer, listen to dreams, or follow intuition?"

I guessed her answer before she said it. "All of the above" she laughed. "And I also followed up by learning things I didn't know, like taking a class in xeriscaping when I needed to learn about which plants to use where in the garden. But it wasn't always like that, I stumbled through life for a long time before really trusting my guidance and intuition."

"Tell me more," I encouraged.

Allison looked thoughtful and took a sip of tea before continuing.

"I believe that I did trust my instincts when I was a child – I think all children do – but I got into trouble for it and stopped listening. There was nothing specific I just knew things. For instance when a particular aunt visited, or a certain friend of my mother's: They would bend down and coo and be very 'nice' with big smiles on their faces; they would say things that sounded right, but didn't feel true to me, I felt they were being deceitful or even lying.

"I had been brought up not to lie, so I couldn't believe that grown ups would lie to me; but I felt it. I'm not sure where I felt it . . . hmmm, right here in my belly, it was a queasy sort of feeling. Sometimes, I would say something to my mommy but she just denied it. Then I would feel bad about mentioning it, because, after all, this was about her sister or her friend. I think I was about four or five at the time. Later, in grade school, I learned to avoid people I didn't like the feel of, but I always seemed to be thrown in with them…"

"What sort of things did you feel that you didn't like?" I interrupted.

"Oh, you know, they seemed too . . ." Allison paused and thought a while.

"I was going to run off a whole long list of things I didn't like about certain people, but I realise now how that doesn't help anyone, and the reality is that most of those characteristics are actually the result of a sensitivity that is ultimately good. It's been thirty-something years since I ever saw those people, and I bet they were having as hard a time with their sensitivities as I was. Instead, I'd like to just think of them for a moment and send them blessings – I don't even know if some of them are still alive, but I hope they will receive these thoughts and feel forgiveness."

We sat together under the tree and my own attention turned to people I, too, had disliked because they seemed "different."

"Labelling anyone 'too anything' is just not fair," she concluded.

"You know, Carly, what we just did there is an example of how guidance works for me. I wasn't planning to spend five minutes in prayerful thought about people I hadn't seen in thirty years, but it happened, it was right in front of me and I followed it. That is how it works, every time. Neither of us can prove whether or not our thoughts were received, but something happened, and I trust it.

"When I was a child I was always being accused of being naive, of believing what everyone said, but that really wasn't what was happening at all. It was the opposite – but it was also true – it's a paradox and I'll try and explain.

"Whenever I heard or read something that just felt 'right' I believed it, and if there was something I needed to do with it, I did it if I could. Like I said before, that often got me into trouble! However, I'd also hear many, many things I didn't believe, but it seemed that most people did and they seemed real enough. I think this part really started when I was about five or six – maybe around when I began school. I learned really fast, and if ever I questioned anything I was basically told to shut up. So, I just carried on learning just to get through tests and exams.

"I think my teachers cared – they liked kids – but I don't think they actually realised that what they were teaching was not just facts and figures, but a *way* of learning, a way to believe. I don't remember when, but I do have a vague recollection of simply resigning to this, sort of giving up. I realise now how I didn't just begin to hide my instincts and intuition, but gave up even believing they were there.

"If the term had been around at the time, I'd say I'd 'given away my power.' Again, sadly, I think many children do this, and then at puberty we magically regain it – or at least glimpse it – and in our attempts to grasp and use it we are accused of rebelling."

At this point, relaxed under the tree, I forgot I had gone along to interview Allison about guidance, simultaneously realising that our entire conversation *was* relevant to this book. I let her continue without asking questions to keep her on track. For Allison, the heart of guidance was about tracking, about following herself and trusting it would lead her in the right direction.

"So, there was this period roughly between age seven and 14 when I absorbed a lot of things at face value, still getting occasional twinges of inner knowing that didn't jibe with what I *was* hearing or being taught. Those twinges were real – literally stomach aches – I had a lot of those as a child, but also it was easier just to let myself go along with it all. I think I was 12 when my sense of myself – my self-esteem – hit an all-time low. Of course, there have been times since, but a lot of things conspired against me then; my parents divorced, I moved with my mother three times in less than two years, my older brother dropped out of high school, things like that.

"I was really floundering, with nothing to hold onto, watching a lot of TV and not even reading. Then, when we moved the third time (I think), there was a swimming pool nearby and I started to go regularly. That fall, I joined the swim team at my new middle school; I loved the water and not having to talk to people. Swimming woke up my body, and ultimately re-awoke my gut instincts and intuition.

"By that age, I'd learned to keep those kind of thoughts to myself, but I did learn to use them to my advantage. Oh, not on things like card games – though that would have been a good idea – I mean like knowing which order we should be in for a relay race. I think our coach, Sue, was also naturally intuitive because she listened to me.

"Carly, you can't imagine how her listening helped me!"

Allison's eyes glazed over a little, and I held the silence between us.

"Coach was the first person who really listened – *really* saw me. I don't know if the others on the team experienced her that way, but I certainly did. She didn't even spend any more time with me than with anyone else, she was just very present and very attentive. She didn't waste words, in fact she was pretty bossy – I suppose that a swim coach is supposed to be like that. Anyway, our team won the school tournament that year, and I think I won for life!

"I swam throughout middle and high school and also got into high diving. Although they both take place in water, they are very different disciplines. Diving taught me – again for life – about patience, timing, and accuracy and about knowing exactly when to take that leap – literally. Have you ever watched the diving in the Olympics? Even there, at the most intense moment in sport, with crowds cheering and millions watching on TV, you are just yourself. I never made it to the Olympics – not even close – but I won the gold medal in a different way.

"I had to be completely and utterly still; no matter what was happening around me, who went before, what their dive looked like, or who was coming after. There is this moment of stillness; it's called 'the zone' now, where every sense is enhanced, where time slows down, where your mind is open, free and alert. For me, I felt extraordinary inner strength and confidence. Not an ego confidence, it's a very aware sense of self – true Self. I still wasn't into spiritual things at the time, so I didn't have the language for it; again just a knowing. The point I'm making here – about the diving – is that standing at the edge of a board all those feet above the water, there is no thought, and yet there is an absolute perfect moment of balance when you know just the right time to dive. You trust your body and its knowing. If you dive before, or after, it doesn't quite cut it. I can feel it now."

I had closed my eyes while Allison was talking and drifted into a slightly altered state, a state of absolute alertness. As she spoke, she radiated a special kind of calm, not peacefulness so much as a sharp, incisive stillness. Everything around us seemed amplified, brighter, and clearer. We both sighed at the same time. Our breath seemed to shift the energy around us and everything softened, coming back to normal, whatever normal was. In Allison's pretty garden life was always vibrant and far from the normal dry of the Southwest.

"I know, we've digressed," she observed, "but that 'gold medal' is really the golden rule I follow about everything. To answer your original question, I might hear an inner voice, in fact I don't really meditate any more, I just kind of get a thought that seems to come from somewhere else. I notice those kinds of thoughts because they don't seem to originate from the usual sea of flotsam and jetsam in my head. So, the next thing I do is pay attention to it.

"Have you ever noticed that whatever you focus on appears to happen? If you're thinking about something a lot, writing about it, or on the phone chatting about it, then later that day someone will call you about that very thing, or you'll reach in your purse and find a note you wrote weeks before that relates to it, or maybe run into someone in the grocery store who has the answer to the question in your head. Some people call this coincidence or synchronicity. It doesn't matter what you call it; whatever we turn our attention towards we give energy to, setting manifestation in motion.

"And that's exactly what happens, especially with these thoughts that come out of left field. I pay attention and then all manner of things start happening that relate, next thing I know . . ."

Allison put down her tea and waved her arms in the air.

"Look around, do I have time to tell this one story? How I came to find this house?"

I hesitated, knowing I really had to be at an appointment with another friend. She caught my look, and we agreed to meet a few days later.

"Just give me a clue," I prompted. "What form of guidance did you use to find the house?"

"I call it 'go' guidance," she grinned. "It moves very, *very* fast."

I knew I'd heard that before somewhere, and then I remembered: It was like Peter Caddy's form of guidance. He never called it guidance, but that's what it was. He was even known to stop in the middle of a cup of coffee when an intuition struck, jump in his car and drive 500 miles without stopping. I promised to tell Allison that story next time we met. In the meantime, I was due to meet a friend who teaches yoga and meditates a lot, so I expected to be immersed in the still, small voice for a while.

We hugged, and agreed to meet under the apricot tree again the following Tuesday.

I slowly got into my car to drive over to meet Yukiko for dinner at our favourite café. There was quite a crowd when I got there. The cafe was hosting one of their Thursday evening lectures, and that evening the topic was about the writing and teachings of Carlos Castaneda. I planned to stay for the talk after dinner, as Castaneda's books had been one of several wonderful inspirations for me about guidance and intuition, and especially about learning how to follow where the energy took me.

A few years ago, on a chilly September evening, I re-read *The Teachings of don Juan*, which I had last read curled up in my cosy Findhorn caravan in 1970. Reading it a second time I was so inspired that I immediately bought Castaneda's second book, *A Separate Reality*, and by spring I had read every one of his books again – this time in chronological order. They formed a strong body of teaching for me about awareness, summoning intent and following spirit. As I walked into the cafe, looking for Yukiko, I noticed my train of thought about Findhorn, Carlos Castaneda and my own life. Findhorn co-founder, Peter Caddy, never used the word "intent," but I believe that's exactly what he did use in order to activate the will to follow spiritual guidance, which he received as inner promptings and intuitive flashes.

Yukiko spotted me before I saw her, which was surprising, because she always stands out in a crowd, partly because of her Japanese features in a town with few people of Far Eastern descent, but also because she is such a sharp dresser. She has lived in fashion capitals Paris, London and Tokyo, plus, her work as a freelance producer and assistant director of television commercials takes her all over the world, offering numerous shopping opportunities along the way. So, before we settled down to our intended topic of conversation, we discussed shoes, but as this is not a book about the best clothing stores in Santa Fe, I will spare you.

We waited to eat until we had finished our conversation. I was aware of her calm centre underneath her vibrant personality, and knowing she had recently returned from a yoga retreat, I expected we would speak about the quiet within and the discipline of stillness.

As it turned out, perhaps inspired by the atmosphere in the cafe and the brilliant colours around us (the walls are painted several shades of orange, vermilion and yellow) our conversation took a different route:

"Intuition for me is a feeling in my body of expansion, not contraction," began Yukiko, opening her arms wide.

"For a long time, I didn't know the difference between intuition and thought; but if something felt good, I acted on it. Other than that, I really didn't think about those sorts of things. Then something happened which totally changed my life.

"I was living in Paris, in my mid-twenties, and working as a professional dancer. It was just before a big performance and I sprained my ankle. I was mortified and needed to do something fast. As well as going to a regular doctor, a friend recommended energy healing, something called *magnetisme*, a kind of magnetic healing. I went to this healer – very suspicious – but had to do something, anything, so I could dance the following week. It worked, I don't remember exactly what she did, but it worked!

"A short while later, I fell ill. Again, I went to doctors, but no one knew what was wrong with me. I was a dancer, supposedly very fit, but I was in pain and could barely climb stairs without labouring for breath. Again, a friend who believed in alternative healing recommended someone to me; she said this woman was a retired, no-nonsense, schoolteacher. That sounded pretty normal to me, so I felt quite reassured and went along for my appointment.

"I hadn't been there five minutes when this 'no-nonsense' woman took out a pendulum and began to wave it over me. I thought here we go again. I was momentarily relieved when she took away the pendulum, but from where I was lying on the table, I could see that she was then waving it over a book – over the index – and then over some plants and rocks on a shelf nearby. When she asked me to hold one of the rocks in my left hand I thought: 'I've got to get out of here.'"

"Do you think that was that your own guidance speaking?" I interrupted.

"No, I think it was pure fear – fear of the unknown – but, of course I didn't know anything then. I stayed anyway. Not sure why, but I did.

"The rock in my left hand started pulsating, and the feeling went all the way up my arm. I was scared at first and felt like throwing it across the room, but I was also fascinated. I literally felt energy pumping up my left arm. I'd had so little energy in my body that this was quite something. Then the energy seemed to wash right through me. '*C'est fini*' the schoolteacher/healer said a few minutes later. I stayed on the table for a while, wondering what had happened, then got up, paid and left. I had so much energy; I ran two metro stops, laughing all the way!

"From that moment on I paid attention to things that seemed intangible, and slowly began to trust that not everything was in a logical sequence. I began to see and converse with the universe in a different way. I began to realise that the universe wasn't just inside my head. When I started to study yoga, I learned about the different bodies we are made up of: the physical, the ethereal, and the causal body – the place where we can access intent."

"So, how do you feel about pendulums now?" I asked, somewhat tongue in cheek.

"Actually, I occasionally use a pendulum to confirm an intuition, but mostly just rely on inner knowing and act from there. My job gives me a chance to practice daily. Now I know that this stuff is not something spooky or weird; in fact it's essential to access our intuition. I find it especially helpful when I'm choosing a team for a commercial shoot. We're on a budget, we have to deliver on time, travel a lot – sometimes three locations for one shoot – and the team has to be very tight. I've learned who will work with a specific team and who won't. It's part of the experience of the job, but also instinct and intuition."

"Do you make a distinction between instinct and intuition?" I wondered.

"No, not really, they are part of the whole; one is confirmation of another, they work together."

We concluded our conversation just as the talk about the teachings of Carlos Castaneda was beginning. I listened attentively, wondering whether intent sprang from the same source as spiritual guidance? As I listened, I felt the origin of intent as a deep, inner knowledge, just as the speaker described how: "In a noble moment of elegance, pure intent can move towards volition, personal intent can align with evolutionary intent." His voice carried a resonance I could taste.

"Intent is not personal will," he reminded us as the evening closed, and I drove home with keen awareness of the power inherent within us, and an infinite universe to be navigated.

Home, I sat down at my computer to enter my notes for this book.

But first I checked my e-mail. There was one from Bruce, my dear friend in California with whom I'd worked on several books as editor, all-around encourager and maker of matzo-ball soup to clear our heads and inspire the creative process on chilly days. Bruce's writing reflects his clear intent to cut through socially accepted half-truths and get to the point – always with humour! A few days earlier, I'd asked him how he recognised the voice of guidance and intuition amid the clamour of the internal dialogue and the voices of reason and 'good advice'?

I have no particular name for information coming through, I do not call it guidance, intuition, or any familiar name. I do call it information, or sometimes visions, voices, knowingness, or body impressions.

It rides close to the other voices of doubt, the ones that say: 'Who do I think I am?' And my fear that I'm being arrogant . . . and then I trust and believe my intent, which is to allow words and insights and observations to pour through without being attached to the information. I do not have to be right. If someone in front of me disagrees, I defer to them and what they see, know, feel and hear.

This ability to not have to be right, or attached to information leaping out of my heart, allows enhanced awareness to pour through. I get out of my own way. It is intrinsic in all creatures. I recognise clearly so-called voices of reason from the outside, or good advice from others. They have a unique quality to them, especially in the voice itself, and how my body receives the information. To me tone of voice reveals more than the content.

Because I usually can recognise the outer world voices of reason – which tend to represent a world that is at constant war – I listen instead to the voices that come from within, from inner authority. And, again, I am not attached to being right. That is the key.

If I feel a clinging to my belief or expression, it becomes a signal that it may not be the truth, but rather a fear. And...

I could sense Bruce hesitating at his computer keyboard and knew he was about to reveal something that was new to him, too.

I know I can lead. I feel the leader within me. The leader being the one that waits – though not as a victim, or wanting things to be different. Instead, if I want change, I change first. Like in a dream I had a few days ago where I heard the words: "First you live out what you ask of others. When living it, there is nothing left to ask."

Simply put, I sense, feel, observe, enjoy and play with it all.

With love, Bruce.

I sat at my keyboard for quite some time before I could begin my notes, the words of his dream resonating inside me: "First you live out what you ask of others. When living it, there is nothing left to ask."

I realised that the task before me, to write a book about spiritual guidance and intuition, would require of me nothing less than living from the source inside myself, the wellspring of guidance.

Chapter 2

The Still Small Voice

"Be still and know that I am God"

In the early 1950's, in a small Sanctuary in Glastonbury, England, Eileen Caddy first heard the unmistakable voice of inner guidance: "Be still and know that I am God." For Eileen in that first moment, the voice did not instantly bring deep peace or anything close to stillness, but many questions and few immediate answers.

Fifty years later, Eileen is recognised as the co-founder of the Findhorn Community with Peter Caddy and Dorothy Maclean. She is revered and respected as one of the most influential women in contemporary spiritual circles, and her simple words of guidance from God have been published and quoted all over the world, bringing comfort and inspiration to millions. Yet, years ago in the quiet of that Glastonbury Sanctuary, Eileen did what most of us have done in times of great need: She pleaded to God for help, guidance and assurance. And, like for many of us, the words she heard in response only furthered her anxiety, because they were not what she expected.

You have taken a very big step in your life. But if you follow My voice all will be well. I have brought you and Peter together for a very special purpose, to do a specific work for Me. You will work as one, and you will realise this more fully as time goes on. There are few who have been brought together in this way. Don't be afraid, for I am with you.

Just a few weeks earlier, Eileen had fallen deeply in love with Peter Caddy – a trusted and well-liked family friend – and had written to her husband requesting a divorce. In an outraged response, her husband had taken full custody of their five children, telling Eileen she could never again set foot in her own home, nor see their children.

Eileen had hoped to discuss their children's needs and custody arrangements, to explain in person what had happened between her and Peter, and to ask for forgiveness and understanding. Instead, she arrived in the quiet Glastonbury Sanctuary on her knees, turning to God as if he was her own father, and expecting Him to embrace her with loving kindness and compassion. She called out from the depths of her heart.

God's words of guidance did little to assure her, yet even then she knew she must follow them. She wondered, too, how God could even condone her actions, as His words implied. Surely God believed His own commandment about adultery? Not only that, didn't God speak only to very special people, like Abraham and Moses? Would he really speak to a woman who had just left her husband and children?

Eileen walked out of that little Sanctuary on Peter's arm, feeling somewhat bewildered. However, in the days and weeks to follow she continued to hear the voice of God, gently reassuring her and calling her "My beloved child," even recognising her resistance, and reminding her that her faith was being tested. She had a choice: To accept the voice, or not. At that time in her life, with so little to cling to, the inner voice became her rock and Eileen learned to discipline herself and to listen in meditation every day. Sometimes she heard other voices, but was always guided to listen for the original voice, the one she had first heard that day, and to let the others fade away. Slowly, but surely, the unmistakable voice of God became her guide and a pattern and picture began to unfold; unseen at the time, today it is a tapestry woven of true love, extraordinary faith, and ever more radiant light.

In later years, she and Peter were to part; yet God told her again that, "All would be very, very well." And, in the spirit of truly unconditional love

– despite the difficulties of parting – Eileen and Peter were able to resolve their differences and come to true peace with one another shortly before he died in a car crash in 1994.

It was many, many years before Eileen was reunited with all of her children. Yet, one-by-one, they came back to her with full and forgiving hearts, and on her 80th birthday all eight of her children (five from her first marriage, and the three sons from her marriage to Peter) came together to celebrate with her.

Despite a shaky start, Eileen's faith in the guidance she received from God just grew and grew. No matter what was happening in her life she was told to "Put God first in everything." There were times when her guidance asked her to make choices; to choose between her relationship with God and her relationship with Peter; to choose between her relationship with God and with her children; even on one occasion to choose between returning to her older children from her first marriage and staying with her younger children from her marriage to Peter! How could anyone, ever, make a decision like that? "Put God first in everything," was always the answer. And, "Let go and Let God."

Be still and Listen. Write down what you hear. Listen, and then act. Discipline is the most basic requirement of the still, small voice. Learning to receive inner guidance is not an end in itself, but rather the beginning of an adventure into spirit, into real life, where trust in God becomes second nature, and where no other voices have room or energy to detract from purpose and intent. In the beginning Eileen resisted the voice time and time again, and was seemingly tested until she fully accepted. There were times when she even resented the voice and all the guidance she had received, believing it had led only to her own downfall and disgrace, and had deeply hurt her children forever. Her circumstances at that time seemed to prove she was right.

In the autumn of 1956 Eileen was living with her six-month-old son, Jonathan, in a remote crofters cottage on the island of Mull in the Scottish Hebrides. Peter was living in Glasgow trying to earn enough money for them to live on for the winter. He sent her a few shillings whenever he could, and whenever the ferry could brave the fierce seas to reach the islands. As autumn turned to bitter winter, she relied mainly on the gifts of basic food and peat for the fire from a neighbour; a young man considered a simpleton by others who brought food from his own meagre table to share with her.

That winter, Eileen experienced the darkest night of the soul, a dark night among many at that time. She felt desperately lonely and very sorry for herself, feeling guilt, shame and anger at her stupidity. In her misery, she even railed against the still, small voice of God, and wished she had never heard it. Only her tiny son's innocent smile and the young neighbour's kindness brought her any hope or joy. However, during the long, dark evenings, she slowly – ever so slowly – began to rebuild her faith.

Wrapped in blankets in the stillness of one night, she recalled the memory of the love of God enfolding her, until her anger subsided and her self-pity imperceptibly lightened. With the dawn, as the light crept through the cracks in the wooden door, she let herself again sink into the arms of God. Cradled like her own baby, she felt the tender love of God soften and embrace her, as bitter tears of resentment changed into the sweet tears of gratitude for all she had. Even though by most people's standards she had next to nothing.

The following morning, she heard God's voice again for the first time in many months, reminding her to count her blessings, and this time she didn't resist it. Instead she did just as He said. She looked around the room at her little son kicking and gurgling happily in his cot, at the fragrant peat logs in a pile by the fireplace, which were a gift from her neighbour. Outside, she heard the sharp calls of the seagulls flying effortlessly and gracefully. She walked up the hill to collect fresh water from the spring behind the cottage and looked out across the island wilderness to the Sound of Iona and at the scudding clouds clearing to blue sky. That day, the voice of guidance, the voice of God, returned fully and strengthened with each passing hour as gratitude opened her heart. Very soon, whether in the midst of a raging storm, or the hardships of a day with only porridge to eat, Eileen found stillness so profound that she knew nothing could ever again disturb it.

Just a few weeks later, Peter wrote to tell her he had a job interview with a hotel chain, and in March 1957, Peter and Eileen were appointed managers of the prestigious Cluny Hill Hotel and Spa in the lovely northern Scottish town, Forres. The townspeople readily accepted them and their growing family, and as they ran the hotel on God's guidance, and the sound spiritual principals of love, kindness and perfection, it soon became one of the most popular and successful destinations in Scotland.

Eileen's story demonstrates the need for absolute faith, for unwavering discipline, for utter obedience and for gratitude. Though gratitude is not the subject of this book, you will see how it weaves in and out of people's lives as they learn to receive guidance and follow intuition. For though guidance and intuition may be our birthright, it is, as Eileen learned, never something to be taken for granted.

Now in her mid-eighties, Eileen still rises well before dawn to sit in the stillness of God's presence, to meditate, and listen to that same inner voice. She no longer lives in a remote crofters cottage or a crowded caravan, but in a comfortable home in the central garden of the Findhorn Community; a home built for her by that same baby son – plus his brothers and friends – whose gurgles lightened her hardened heart almost fifty years earlier.

She takes a long, hot bath each morning before leaving the warmth of her house for the simple, cedar wood Sanctuary at the heart of the Community; dressing elegantly and warmly and savouring a good hot cup of tea before stepping out into the chill morning air.

Last January, on a particularly icy morning, my friend Karin had a chance to sit with Eileen during her early meditation, experiencing her presence and witnessing her routine:

> Wrapping herself in a warm coat, she walks the few yards towards the Sanctuary, leaving the first footsteps in the newly fallen snow around her house. Everything around her is totally silent, the Community Centre opposite her house is empty, and she seems to be the only person around at this time on a winter's morning. On the way to the Sanctuary she passes the caravan she lived in forty years earlier; the caravan she left at the same time every morning for the same purpose as today, to listen to her still small voice, the voice she recognises as God's words.

However, even at this early hour she is not the first one in the Sanctuary. A small, smiling Japanese woman, who Eileen calls 'her little angel,' has opened the curtains, turned up the heating, and lit the candle in the centre which casts a soft light into the room. The two women smile at each other, obviously very grateful for one-another's presence.

For the next half hour, these two women sit with their eyes closed in silent meditation, each with her own intimate, inner experience. And then there come small sounds from outside, more footprints in the snow, the creaking of floorboards, and a soft cough. One by one, other people are arriving to join the meditation.

For Eileen, this has been a daily ritual for forty years. For me, it is the first time I have joined this very early morning time of silent contemplation, where the only sound comes from the breath of the dozen people now in the room. I slide softly into nothingness and for a while there are no thoughts and no feelings.

Perhaps an hour later, I become aware once more of my body sitting heavily on the chair and I feel wet tears rolling down my cheeks – from where they came I do not know. I feel only an inner peace."

Karin's inner peace is the beginning of turning inward to the essential Self and to listening to the voice of God. Though some people, like Eileen, hear a clear, unmistakable voice, for many others the peace is simply a place of deep, sweet relaxation into a universal pool of love and heightened consciousness; for others it is a time of inner silent rest from the incessant chatter of the mind.

Although I don't receive guidance through the still, small voice of God, I do remember the first time I realised in a meditation that my thoughts were separate from me. I wasn't so much having them, as *watching* them, and in so doing realised that they were quite separate from my essential, quiet self. It was in the Sanctuary at Cluny Hill, where, wrapped in a cosy, yellow blanket, I realised, astonished, how my thoughts were there but they weren't bothering me. I had an image of them as birds flying from tree-to-tree, some open winged in flight, some perched chattering to others on branches, and some like crows or rooks squawking and screeching loudly. They didn't bother me and I didn't feel the need to do anything with them. I just watched them.

It is from this place that the still, small voice arises, and why I personally don't hear it at those times, I do not know, though I am blessed to receive guidance in other ways. Peter Caddy also did not hear the still small voice – except on one most significant occasion.

It was October 1952 and he was stationed in the Middle East, where he took the opportunity to visit the holy sites in Jerusalem. It was sunset, and Peter was resting on a hill overlooking the city, thinking about nothing in particular – certainly not meditating – when quite out of the blue he clearly heard in his head the words: "Eileen is your other half." He was astonished. He had met Eileen only a few times and liked and respected her very much, but had never thought about her in a romantic way. Besides, she was married with five children to one of his friends and colleagues!

He dismissed the idea as ridiculous. However, he could not dismiss the clarity with which he heard the voice, so decided that next time he saw Eileen he would tell her how God had said they were soul halves, just to see what she thought! A few months later while at a dinner party he managed to get a moment alone with Eileen and confessed that God said they were to be together. Eileen's first response was laughter. But seeing how Peter was so clear and sincere, she advised that if it was to be so, then God would take care of the details. To let be what would be.

Eileen's trust in waiting and Peter's extraordinary ability to seize the moment formed the basis of their partnership and marriage, and laid the foundation of vision and action upon which the Findhorn community unfolded.

Chapter 3

HANGING ON TO YOUR HAT: GUIDANCE IN ACTION

"When you put your hand in God's, hold on to your hat with the other hand"
[often quoted by Peter Caddy]

Peter Caddy tells some pretty amazing stories about how he learned to follow intuition and inner guidance at a moment's notice. Peter didn't sit still very often and rarely meditated; his way of receiving guidance was about as opposite to Eileen's as you could imagine. Community members often regarded (for better or worse) Peter and Eileen as father and mother figures and certainly in the early days they fitted their gender roles: Eileen was considered more receptive and open, while Peter was regarded as more aggressive and impulsive. Later, life brought them both experiences to balance their roles. For the formative years of the Findhorn Community though, the role-playing and balance was perfect.

I was lucky and blessed to live at Findhorn in the very early years of the community. In the winter of 1970, there were about sixty of us living in the caravans and bungalows dotted around the Findhorn Bay Caravan Park. Cluny Hill was still operating as a hotel in the nearby town of Forres, and though Eileen received regular Word from God that she and Peter would one day "return to Cluny," that day was to be five years away.

Every evening, all sixty or so of us would dress up for dinner, which was served in the Community Centre's dining room. Eileen would come over and, assisted by her dear friend, Joanie Hartnell Beavis, cooked many of the utterly delicious community meals; except when potter, Brian, concocted one of his fabulous curries, or when elder, Joan, served Scalloped Potatoes au Gratin; when Jenny made spicy nut loaf with a baby on her back, or dancer, Zanni, offered her incomparable Spaghetti Bolognese. Sunday was Peter's day in the kitchen. He would don an apron to make sixty perfect cheese or mushroom omelettes. However, I am digressing (but then no book on guidance could possibly be complete without some mention of food – are cooks not some of the most intuitively guided and inspired people on the planet?)

After dinner, replete with dessert such as bread pudding, apple crumble with custard, or chocolate mousse made with fresh cream, we would clear off the tables, move the chairs, sweep up a bit, and settle down for the evening to listen to Peter's stories. He was a master storyteller. He would regale us with tales of his meeting with his first spiritual teacher when he was just nineteen years old – a Rosicrucian teacher of the Crotona Fellowship called Dr. Sullivan; of his travels in the Himalayas, the Holy Land, and the Far East as Catering Officer in the RAF during and after World War II; and of the magical, formative days of the community and all the adventures and misadventures leading up to the founding of Findhorn. No one ever missed these evenings. Peter had everyone gripped and even if we'd heard the story before we all knew there would be a new take, a little embellishment here or there, or an insight just waiting to happen.

Dr. Sullivan – under the spiritual name of Aureolis – had taught Peter the potency of positive thought and he told him that each individual had the power to change the world. Aureolis taught how by thinking you direct your life into expression, and that what you believe to be true moulds your destiny; how through thought you either consciously or unconsciously become your own creator. Under Dr. Sullivan, Peter learned the art of "soul science," which was to lay the foundation for his future life and especially how he responded to his growing intuition.

affix
stamp
here

to:

FINDHORN PRESS

305a The Park
Findhorn
Forres IV36 3TE
Scotland, Great Britain

Peter Caddy's brand of intuition was unique. Though he would always say he didn't hear voices or see visions, he certainly heard something: a knowing so clear he didn't question it. And it was central to Peter's life and mission – he learned to trust his intuition so completely and instantly that if he paused to question it he missed it.

Many years before Peter Caddy was born, way back in 1899, a man called Fra Elbertus Hubbard wrote a tiny book in just one hour. He said: "It leaped hot from my heart." Called *Message to Garcia*, it told the story of how a man called Rowan had "gone alone and done the thing," he had carried a vital message from McKinley to General Garcia (somewhere in Cuba) during the war between the United States and Spain in the late 19th Century. Fra Elbertus's thirty four-page booklet sold forty million copies around the world and was translated into dozens of languages – absolutely unprecedented in the publishing world in those days! I mention this here because the message of that book is the same message Peter Caddy later taught: The hero is the man who does his work; when you receive the Word, do not hesitate or question, and do not pass the buck. "Go alone and do the thing," no matter what.

Rowan delivered the message with no question, and Fra Elbertus wrote the book with unquestionable inner directive, faith and discipline of spirit. Those two actions changed the course of world history. And Peter Caddy's life and stories followed the exact same tone: When something "leaped hot from his heart" he saw it as an unmistakable sign to act, without hesitation and without question. However, that hadn't always been the case.

One day, while in a cafe in Oban, on the west coast of Scotland, enjoying a cup of tea with Eileen and his former wife and spiritual teacher, Sheena, Peter had a sudden inner prompting to go immediately down to Hampshire in the south of England. He didn't hesitate – he didn't even finish his cup of tea. Some months earlier, Sheena had chided Peter for not immediately following his intuition and he had paid heed. They had been relaxing and brewing coffee together when Peter got a prompting to go see a particular person, a man called Jack. The coffee was still brewing, so Peter waited to drink a cup before leaving. Just before he left, Sheena shocked Peter by telling him she thought Jack had a gun and was about to kill himself, and that Peter's hesitation had probably cost his friend his life. Fortunately, that story was not true; Sheena was being mischievous and had made up the story to drill into Peter the absolute necessity of following intuition instantly.

So, that afternoon in Oban, Peter put down his cup of tea and took off with hardly enough money in his pocket to even get a bus to the next town. Stepping outside he spotted a fancy car on the high street and thumbed a lift to the next village, only to discover the driver was actually going all the way to London! And to top it all, she even had a picnic basket on the back seat packed for the trip, among its contents a whole roast chicken.

On his return journey north, Peter again followed his intuition unfailingly, including jumping out of a lorry at traffic lights upon spotting a girl in a red sports car. For a split second he worried that asking her for a lift was a bit of a cheek, but chose to ignore his rational mind and only seconds before the lights changed asked if she was possibly going to Scotch Corner. Sure enough she was and, yes, she even had a delicious assortment of sandwiches packed in a cooler and a large flask of hot coffee for the trip.

Peter's stories about following his intuition abounded, whether about hitchhiking or space brothers; meeting St. Germain, the Master of the Seventh Ray; or knowing whether or not someone was meant to live in the community. Those long, dark winter evenings in the Community Centre listening to Peter had an impact on everyone, and upon reflection I cannot imagine a better way to have learnt the basic principles of positive thought, following intuition and summoning inner discipline. Peter's tales – however tall – would have us either rollicking with laughter or perching on the edges of our seats. Many of the stories I'd had the privilege to hear firsthand on those winter nights can be found in *In Perfect Timing*, Peter's autobiography, which was published in 1996, two years after his death in a car crash in Germany.

Every story held a lesson in following intuition, no matter how strange; there was one particular tale that touched me then, and now, because within it I recognised a thread weaving magically through my own life. It was a story about Peter's first meeting with a remarkable woman called Liebie Pugh, in St. Annes on Sea, Lancashire. She was the founder of a group called Universal Link and a channel for The All-Knowing One – also known as Limitless Love and Truth – a Being of incredible love and wisdom overlighting the unfolding of spiritual work in Britain at that time.

In his autobiography Peter tells of how he was on his way to Glastonbury one August Bank Holiday weekend with Dorothy Maclean and their American friend, Naomi:

> Our first stop was in Edinburgh to take a basket of compost-grown fruit and vegetables to the Countess of Mayo . . . a legendary worker for the Light, and many years ahead of her time.

On that visit to her home, Peter met a friend of Lady Mayo's who was on her way down to St. Annes to connect with Liebie Pugh and her group and who needed a lift down south.

> We arrived in St. Annes late the next day . . . and intended to leave, but at the last moment decided to stay and meet Liebie. First, however, we had to confront a guardian on the gate: Joan Hartnell-Beavis, Liebie's secretary and treasurer who lived in the flat next door and was obviously devoted to her. When we arrived she said that Liebie was quite tired and that it was long past her meal time; we could only have an appointment the next day. I replied that we had to go to Glastonbury in the morning and Joanie – as we came to know her – relented.
>
> Liebie Pugh had a remarkable face, like a Tibetan's, and her features seemed neither male nor female, neither oriental nor occidental, but had elements of all. She took my hands, and the first words she said were, "St. Germain." She recognised that I had a strong link with the Master of the Seventh Ray.

Peter, Dorothy and Naomi continued on their journey to Glastonbury knowing they would see Liebie and Joanie again, and that St. Annes would be a regular stopping point on their journeys to visit and link up the special places of spiritual power around Britain. When Liebie died a couple of years later, Joanie came to live at Findhorn and became Eileen's closest friend and confidant as well as Treasurer of the Findhorn Trust.

The night in the Community Centre when I first heard Peter tell that story held special significance for me, confirming how my own life was definitely guided by Spirit. Shortly before Peter's meeting with Liebie, I had moved with my parents and sister to Blackpool, only a few miles away from St. Annes on Sea. In fact, in the summer of 1965, when the Universal Link group was regularly meditating in St. George's Square, I was attending night classes in a nearby college and Liebie and Joanie's flats were directly across from the bus stop where I waited each evening. Not only that, but on later visits to Lancashire, Peter regularly called on another man of spiritual wisdom who owned a private sanctuary on the very corner of the street where I lived! Deep into my own spiritual search, that house had always intrigued me with its small sign saying "Sanctuary."

Hearing Peter's story for the first time, I wondered why I hadn't ever knocked on the sanctuary door or felt the presence of Limitless Love and Truth illuminating the house by the bus stop in St. Annes? But I came to realise it was all about timing. I had several of my own (quite wonderful) experiences to go through before I would meet Peter, Dorothy and Eileen, and sure enough it was exactly five years later that Findhorn called me through Spirit; a call I heeded without hesitation.

Just before my arrival – on August Bank Holiday, 1970 – David Spangler, a young man of great wisdom and sensitivity had arrived from America. Soon after his arrival he attuned to the presence of Limitless Love and Truth, over lighting and seeding itself into the fabric of the Findhorn Community. During the last weeks of August and in early September, Limitless Love and Truth, through David, revealed its powerful and gentle presence directly to our open hearts and minds. It was clear to me, beyond a shadow of a doubt, that my own spiritual calling was being met; especially so when my first job in the community was to transcribe several of the tapes from those extraordinary sessions!

David had come to Findhorn with his partner, Myrtle Glines, and brought to the community yet another form of receiving spiritual guidance. Indeed, the three founders and other people of great influence upon the fledgling community each brought with them very different examples of guidance. One of the community's great attractions was the freshness of being able to follow many paths, or one's own, not necessarily having to abide by the rules and order of a guru or single teacher.

So, along with David Spangler came a strengthening within the entire community of the inner link with a vast presence of universal love. Back in Christmas 1967, through Liebie in St. Annes, Limitless Love and Truth had revealed: "My universal revelation through the medium of nuclear evolution is complete . . . the whole of nuclear energy is Me . . . the Universal Love flow is increasing. All is well."

Peter, and others associated with Findhorn, understood this message to mean that universal love had fully penetrated the nuclear – cellular structure – of all matter. At this time Eileen confirmed through guidance:

> You will be able to live more by the Spirit than you have done and the things of the world will fade away and have no place in your life . . . You will become consciously aware of The Christ Presence, of the Christ Love . . . This tremendous release of Cosmic Power has awakened within each one of you something that has been lying dormant for a very long time and something quite wonderful has begun to germinate within. This release of cosmic energy, power, vibration and radiation . . . is creating tremendous changes in mankind and in the world structure. Nothing can ever be the same again.

David Spangler spoke of this during a lecture he gave to the community that summer, entitled Communication and Communion:

> Through the impact on human conscious evolution made by nuclear research, we have been given a new world view of a universe that is not form but something essentially much subtler and more powerful – an energy, a spirit, that is everywhere present and active. For the first time, we can appreciate the reality of a Presence and an Awareness that states, 'I AM in all things. I AM the Life of all.' Whether we call this God, The Christ, Limitless Love and Truth, or whatever, it makes no difference. Through nuclear research and the evolution of such research, we have been forced to recognise the reality and the power of the unseen, unified energy world that links us all together in oneness. This ceases to be a superstition and becomes a most potent, living realisation and reality.

"This nuclear revelation gives us yet another insight: all that exists apparently outside of us exists within us as well. We seem to be separated from each other and from the world by our physical form and consciousness, but in the new understanding of reality and unified energy field, there actually is no real separation. Oneness is the reality."

When David first attuned to Limitless Love and Truth and guidance was sought regarding sharing the words and energy of this universal presence, Limitless Love and Truth offered:

Proclaim that I AM a living revelation, that I am functioning through this Centre, not in competition with any other centre nor with anything that has been, but that I AM the Spirit of the new and of growth. I will not remain static. I will not remain with what has been. I will not remain according to the wishes of man. I AM Truth. I am not wishful thinking.

This is My Centre. This is My Body. It is not all of Me, for I AM the new heaven and the new earth. I reveal Myself through you, through group revelation, yet I still dwell and reveal Myself through single men and women who have yet to be linked or who may be special messengers performing a special task. But all shall be linked together, for I have sounded My call and none who are of Me can resist it, but will come joyously to merge with what I AM within themselves and in their sharing with others who are of Me in my revealed state."

The words and the energy stimulated my soul, my inner vision and my determination to find my place within this great cosmic dance. At times, my daily life at Findhorn seemed almost mundane; all of us were engaged in the active building of a physical community that by this time was drawing hundreds of people. I heeded Eileen's guidance; immersed myself in the magnificent presence of Limitless Love, and listened inwardly for my own voice. It became clear that my particular "voice" was one that spoke best through action, that my guidance worked more like Peter's than Eileen's, though I continued to take time to sit in meditation or to walk in nature. Most especially, I had wonderful tea breaks with Dorothy Maclean in her tiny caravan where I gleaned just a hint from her of the love and joy to be found in the world of the Devas.

Chapter 4

SHIMMERING AND SHINING

"There is little other than guidance. It is an integration of all bodies—body, mind and spirit."

[Nura]

While writing this book, I was blessed to spend several days with Dorothy Maclean when she visited New Mexico. Through our conversations and from participating in her seminar on inner listening, I learned aspects of the origins of the Findhorn community previously unknown to me – in particular the source of the inner guidance from which Dorothy later opened to the Angelic realm, which she called the Devas. What I learned and understood showed me more clearly than ever that the source of guidance is always God, Great Spirit, or whatever word you choose. I was reminded that, first and foremost, recognising and acknowledging the wholeness of our own Being allows us access to guidance in its myriad forms; to "Put God first, and all else shall follow."

In this chapter I will share with you a brief synopsis of the birth of the Findhorn Community and the decade prior – the true foundation of faith and guidance upon which Findhorn was built – a living example of inner listening and outer action.

In November 1962, Peter and Eileen Caddy, with three growing boys, and their long-time colleague, Dorothy Maclean, set up their summer holiday caravan in a hollow in the Findhorn Bay Caravan Park. The friends expected to spend the winter there and hoped to be re-hired in the spring at the nearby Cluny Hill Hotel, which they had successfully managed for several years. However, in the spring the hotel opened without them and their inner guidance told them to stay in the caravan park. Despite their best efforts, neither Peter nor Dorothy could find work in town, but regardless they settled down to create a cosy home. A wooden annex was built onto the caravan for Dorothy, and as winter darkness enfolded the little home they gathered together each evening around a bright, coke-burning stove to share meals, help the boys with homework, and share their spiritual guidance with one another.

Long before managing Cluny Hill Hotel, the three friends had spent many years studying under the wise counsel of Sheena, Peter's former wife, who made real to them – through her own example – the loving, living presence of the inner God. Her role was almost one of midwife, for the birth of the Christ within. During that period, Dorothy, Eileen and Peter learned and experienced – often through tests of faith – that God truly was within and accessible. Each of them began to receive inner guidance in a different way: Eileen received visions and heard words which she wrote down; Peter's guidance came through action and being absolutely in the present moment; and Dorothy experienced a silent attunement with God and translated her experiences into her own words.

Sheena suggested that Dorothy and Eileen attune regularly to the God within, no matter what else was happening around them. This helped them to develop an extraordinary discipline and the ability to tap into the God source under any circumstances. All three learned to put God first in everything; they were challenged and tested on numerous occasions until they really *got it* and built up an invincible faith in spiritual guidance and clear intuition. Dorothy aimed to remember God on the hour, every hour, and though she usually forgot, she continued her thrice-daily meditations and in particular, the midday meditation in her office brought great joy.

This was early in the 1950's, thus for ten years before the founding of Findhorn, Eileen and Dorothy were attuning to God within. Shortly after her first experience with God, Dorothy received guidance to "Stop, listen and write." In the beginning, she censored what she received, because she didn't understand or trust the process, but when Sheena confirmed that what she was receiving and writing was the truth, Dorothy stopped censoring and freely wrote down all her feelings and impressions. She was receiving wonderfully inspiring thoughts and feelings and writing her impressions down opened up a whole new way of attuning to inner silence and understanding the co-creative process with God. Dorothy learned that she needed to be in a state of wholeness, clarity and love before putting anything on paper. At first, she resisted the arduous discipline of getting up early to do this – when she would have preferred to sleep – however, her times of stillness soon became the most joyous of her day.

In the beginning Dorothy censored what she received, because she didn't understand or trust the process, but when Sheena confirmed that what she was receiving and writing was the truth, she stopped the censoring and freely wrote down all her feelings and impressions. She learned to return to the inner state of love, peace, joy, and truth – a place deeper than her usual thoughts – which became familiar to her. It became easier to enter the sacred place where her usual emotions were not present; if they were, she knew she wasn't there!

Very soon, her thrice-daily sittings became a spring from which great joy and peace flowed endlessly, and she couldn't imagine how earlier she had found such times to be burdensome; these were the very best moments of each day. Message after uncensored message was filled with bubbling joy and the great love of God as Dorothy broke free from the constraints of both the conscious and the unconscious mind and listened inwardly. "Listen to my shimmering thought life," she wrote, "to my elfin mind." Dorothy was enraptured by the joy of it all. One day, God said: "Brush your teeth with me," which caused her to laugh out loud in the midst of her meditation; but from then on she tried to remember God whenever she brushed her teeth. The messages gradually became deeper and even more loving, as well as instructive and practical.

By the time they arrived at Findhorn, Eileen and Dorothy were well practiced in the discipline of turning within, writing down the words or impressions they received and following their guidance implicitly. One day, some months after moving to the caravan park, Dorothy received an inner directive to "Feel into the nature forces." She figured that would be a breeze; spring was coming and she loved to hike across the dunes to Burghead Bay and ramble in the forest at the beautiful Randolph's Leap, where the Rivers Findhorn and Divie meet.

However, when she went within the following day, she sensed for the very first time the sheer enormity of the power of nature. She was told: "Everything in nature has an ensouling intelligence: clouds, rain, vegetables…" She was also told that she was to "Harmonise with the essence of nature." At first it seemed nonsense to her that a brainless vegetable could have intelligence and anyway, even if it did how could she contact it? She ignored her instructions, but not for long. Shortly afterwards, during another meditation, she experienced being in such a stream of power that she realised that, yes, she could try and attune to even a brainless vegetable!

Choosing her favourite, the garden pea, she considered what its essence was from the outer form that she knew, and immediately was in touch with that essence. The garden pea communicated a message in the same way she received sacred wisdom from within, and Dorothy put it into words. She was told that even though humans were great beings of light, they were not using their wholeness, and that when they did, they could co-operate consciously with nature and help the planet.

Dorothy became aware that she was communicating with the ensouling intelligence of the garden pea species, not with a single plant. She understood that all plants have soul groups, and that she was attuning to the soul level of all the garden peas in the world; this was a great planetary being and it wanted to connect with and attune to Dorothy! They had been waiting to contact humans and were more than willing to co-operate in creating heaven on earth. From her own God-self, she could attune into the wholeness, the God-self, of anything and receive its wisdom.

As she emerged from that first experience of oneness with nature, Dorothy realised it was her attunement with her own wholeness – her soul essence – that had allowed her to connect with the wholeness of the plant kingdom. Once she was in that clear place she recognized as God within, she could go where she chose.

Dorothy's inner connection with the souls of different species was a subset of her connection with her own divinity. She attuned first with her wholeness, and from there with the wholeness of the architects of the nature kingdom. She learned that beings of nature are complex and would present diverse aspects of themselves as needed through their essence. There was no sense of separation between her consciousness and the consciousness of the plant's angelic or soul essence: rather it was simply the recognition and joining of one divine essence (human) with another divine essence (plant). Dorothy sensed the essence as a formless energy field; the closest description of it was Angelic. However, for the most part, the word angel didn't fit because traditional angels are not formless and are shown with harps and wings – and these definitely had neither! Dorothy remembered the Sanskrit word Deva (meaning shining one) and decided this description fitted better.

When Peter Caddy first heard that Dorothy had contacted the soul essence of a vegetable he got very excited and immediately made a list of questions for Dorothy to ask the garden vegetables . . . and kept her busy for years! Peter expanded their garden, first with vegetables and later with flowers. Very soon, Dorothy was busy attuning to Devas of every kind and the garden benefited thanks to all manner of help on how and when to plant, even how to deal with rats and moles – and cutworms (that story in just a moment).

Shortly after her first contact with the garden pea, Dorothy became aware of a very expansive Being which appeared to be in charge of the life of all the land upon which they were living –she named this Being the Landscape Angel. She realised later that it was a kind of local representative of the Angel of the Planet; it gave advice on the growth of the garden, on inner energies, on how humans fit into the whole, and also acted as an intermediary for other Angelic Beings. Dorothy gradually understood that the Devas held the blueprint for the pattern, shape, design, and growth of their particular plant species and directed its course and timing. She compared this to an architect who designs the plans for a building, and who later passes on those plans to the building contractor and his workers – in this case the nature spirits or elementals – who do the actual construction and work under the jurisdiction of the architect or Deva.

Fed up with the damage caused by cutworms, which were busy chomping away at the cabbage rootlets, Peter asked Dorothy to get advice from the Devas about how to get rid of the worms. She first asked the Landscape Angel, who replied that the Deva's job was to enhance life, not to get rid of it! Instead she was advised to give love to the cabbages and to think of the sick plants as healthy and vigorous, and to give them as much outer sustenance as possible. Through this love and attention, the cabbages became so healthy the cutworms no longer attacked them.

The Devas did not instruct or command, but instead allowed their knowledge to become known so that it was as close as Dorothy's own skin; sharing their knowledge, qualities and love. Learning how to love, to stay in the God presence of her wholeness, was key to her receptivity and guidance. One day she had to pick off woolly caterpillars, which were eating the gooseberry bushes; she carefully removed them one-by-one, placing them in a jam jar, which she later emptied onto the compost heap for the birds to eat. She hated to touch creepy crawlies. To her dismay, the following morning there was even more of them: Brother, sister and cousin caterpillars were munching away for all they were worth on the crisp and tasty gooseberry leaves.

Frustrated, Dorothy suddenly realised she was working with the caterpillars using hate rather than love, whereas the whole point of her life was to learn to be more loving. The next day she picked off a few of them with love in her heart, explaining to them exactly why the gooseberries were needed and asking for co-operation. To her amazement and relief they all vanished and never returned to that particular gooseberry patch. Love, she was reminded again, was the most basic element of all. As time went by, Dorothy learned to communicate with the Angelic realms of the mineral, animal and human kingdom by this same method.

Dorothy also learned that one has to be on the same level of spirit as whatever or whoever one is contacting. If one feels either inferior or superior, the contact is only tentative and cannot be complete. From our God-self there is equality with the God-self of everything. Love is the portal, the doorway to all the realms of life and nature, and most especially the portal to one's own true Self, to wonder and awe and beauty. From that day on, Dorothy's ability to go straight to the soul essence of any plant was enhanced as she entered the purity of her own loving wholeness. There were days or times when she found it harder to attune to normal life, but when she looked within, she soon realised she was out of harmony with her own God self. Restoring that harmony and opening her heart, giving thanks, and clearing her mind of doubt and worry was always the key to clear and effortless communication and co-operation.

In 1965, another extraordinary piece of magic from the world of spirit wove its way into the essence of Findhorn; those who listened and were attuned to its message heard another voice of guidance.

On Peter Caddy's ever-more-frequent trips south to Glastonbury and other centres of ancient spiritual power and beauty, he often stayed over in Edinburgh. On one such evening, he was introduced to a softly spoken gentleman called Robert Ogilvie Crombie – known to his friends as Roc. Peter had noticed Roc before at various gatherings; he appeared to be a man who stayed in the background, saying little, but with an air of wisdom and quiet authority. He also always had a twinkle in his eye as if to say that nothing should be taken too seriously.

Peter wrote of his first impressions of Roc:

> I became very interested in him and enquired into his background. Roc was a man with many talents: He had been a radio operator on a boat in the English Channel during World War I, had studied music at university and was an

accomplished pianist and an actor. He was also trained as a scientist, but a congenital heart defect prevented him from taking full-time employment; although born and raised in Edinburgh, he was advised by his doctors during World War II to live in the country, which he did, spending ten years in an isolated cottage nine miles from Perth. He was supported by an invalid's pension from the State and developed a close rapport with nature, as well as devoting himself to studying a wide range of scientific, philosophical and spiritual subjects. He now lived frugally in an immaculate Edinburgh flat whose walls were lined with thousands of books, and despite his heart condition he regularly swam in the icy sea. In all, he was an extraordinary man with whom I soon developed a close rapport.

Peter was intrigued as to why Roc attended gatherings about such matters as UFO's and was told by a mutual friend that Roc – being a scientist – had really wanted nothing to do with space beings, but quite recently had had several encounters with various other-worldly beings and wanted to find out more. "It was as if a curtain had been drawn open into other dimensions," wrote Peter:

They were not visions, such as Eileen and other sensitives perceived, but for Roc actual experiences of an alternate reality that overlaid, yet seemed as natural as the world around us. The most exciting of these, as far as our work at Findhorn was concerned, occurred in March 1966, shortly before Roc paid us his first visit. He was sitting with his back to a tree one sunny afternoon in Edinburgh's beautiful Royal Botanic Gardens when, to his astonishment, he saw dancing before him a little faun straight out of Greek mythology; it seemed as real and solid as the other people in the gardens. The faun was as amazed as Roc that he could see him, and the two were soon in conversation.

Whether Roc and the faun spoke to one another aloud or mentally, not even Roc could discern.

Kurmos (as the faun was called) was a nature spirit, one of the elemental beings responsible for helping individual plants grow to the overall blueprint held by the Deva of their species . . . Kurmos himself was concerned with helping the growth of trees in the park.

Roc later explained that these elemental beings are actually whirls or vortices of energy that can appear to human eyes . . . in the archetypal forms of fauns, elves, sprites, etc., as that is the easiest way for our brains to interpret the sensory information. Some people see them only as little bursts of light or colour.

Kurmos and Roc had several meetings after that, either in the gardens or in Roc's flat, and Roc learned much about the relationship between the human and nature kingdoms, particularly the danger of humans continuing to abuse, pollute and exploit the natural world. If the nature spirits withdrew their energy as a result, it would have a disastrous effect on all life. This warning was sounded even more clearly a month later when Roc had the awesome experience of meeting the great being and overlord of all the nature spirits – Pan, the traditional god of woodlands and the countryside.

Roc's legendary meeting with Pan is told in full in *The Findhorn Garden* (book) and *Conversations with Pan* (audiotape); suffice to say that Roc's deepening connection with the unseen worlds was to have a profound affect on the unfolding Findhorn Community, and ultimately Roc became the guardian and protector on the inner planes of the community as it grew in both numbers and fame. Some likened him to the great wizard, Merlin, and although he always seemed quiet and even self-effacing, there was no mistaking the twinkle in his kind eyes and the way they would sometimes flash fire when he sensed that his beloved world of nature was threatened.

My great personal memory of Roc was his flawless playing of Messiaen, Satie, or Debussy on the baby grand piano in the Findhorn Sanctuary. Before a piano recital, Roc would give a short lecture about the relationship between music and nature, and the particular pieces, or keys of music, which certain nature spirits resonated with. In particular, the compositions of Olivier Messiaen, Roc said, helped to break up old patterns and thought forms to make way for new energy. In late February 1975, I needed a ride to near Edinburgh, and was offered a lift by a friend of Roc's who was taking him to Loch Tay. It was the only time I ever had for quiet and personal conversation with him. Two weeks later, following a short illness, he died peacefully at his friend's home. Findhorn lost its great protector and mentor, but Roc's gifts to the community will live on forever.

PART TWO

WEAVING THE WORLDS

Chapter 5

The Edge Between Intuition and Reason

"Being in the right place at the right time is one thing – but also be prepared. Plan to include the unexpected and you're one step ahead."
[Author unknown]

During my childhood, and especially in my teens, I often felt out of place in the world, finding it easier much of the time to stay in my imaginative world where I had friends and where I was always understood and seen. The world "out there" seemed too structured and stiff, with people rushing about being busy and missing the nuances of life, which to me *were* life. Through school, college, work and social expectations, however, I began to emerge into the so-called normal world and to hone my intellect and reasoning mind quite well.

Through the sciences, metaphysics and especially through science fiction – my reading genre of choice – I found a way to comfortably live with both my innate intuitive powers and my curious mind. In fact, by the time I discovered the Findhorn Community at the age of twenty-two, I saw how the worlds that had appeared so separate in my youth were in fact one glorious interactive world. I relaxed into myself and began to have fun for the first time in my life!

Of course, I was also among my peers for the first time, too, people who were all learning to bridge the apparent gap between intuition and reason, and between spirit and structure. I remember early on having a conversation with a friend whose words struck such a chord that I wrote them down. A small, untidy folder of quotes from that time has followed me around the world from then on; I take them out and read them about every ten years. Recalling her face, but not her name, I remember we were talking about the creative edge between planning, spontaneity and synchronicity.

Hers was the quote at the top of this page: "Being in the right place at the right time is one thing – but also be prepared. Plan to include the unexpected and you're one step ahead."

I don't recall my response, but my life's experiences since that time have proved this again and again as I have practiced to seamlessly weave the worlds and, ultimately, find the still point in the centre. The Navajo weavers of northwestern New Mexico and Arizona weave one seemingly out of place thread through the intricate traditional pattern of their beautiful rugs and blankets. The one thread is called a spirit line, which runs all the way from the top edge of the blanket to the bottom edge. Whenever I see it, the spirit line reminds me to let Spirit weave through my life, even if it looks odd and seems to break the pattern. Guidance, especially, comes in the moment we break the pattern; when we make space for surprise and for mystery; when we are willing to go to the edge; when we surrender – even when we believe we cannot.

As I was completing the above paragraph, the phone rang and my son, Joss, ran to answer it.

"Hi, Dad!" I overheard him say.

"When are you coming over? Thirty minutes? OK. That's about one o'clock. OK."

My ex-husband, Diego, arrived a couple of hours later with a big bag of potato chips for Joss and an electric drill in his hand. Unknown to me,

Joss had asked him to fix something in his room. "Daddy can fix anything," has been our son's mantra since he was a toddler and neither divorce nor living in two homes had phased Joss's appreciation and awe of his dad's handyman skills. I am simply grateful for the help and the hard work we had done over the years to be at ease in each other's presence and in co-parenting our two children.

I made a pot of British Rail (a name we had coined years before for regular, but rather weak black tea served every morning on the trains) and remembered that I had yet to interview Diego for the book.

After fixing Joss's curtain rail, we settled down in the sunroom with our tea and Diego began with his story:

"My guidance process has been quite profound throughout my life. One of the first real times I had to depend on my intuition was in Air Traffic Control."

Diego had been an FAA licensed air traffic controller for the US military and NATO in the early seventies, and though I'd heard his stories many times, he always had a new one to tell. Joss hovered in the doorway, listening intently.

"I remember my very first day as a trainee. I was in shock! I walked into the control tower and couldn't believe how these guys could respond to all the air traffic – much less *control* it. There was a wall of sound; must have been twelve radio channels with pilots all talking at once. I couldn't distinguish one voice from another and wondered how on earth they could understand anything. I thought I'd made a huge mistake; I didn't know how I was ever going to survive this job. I stood there aghast thinking, 'How did I sign up for this, and how can I get out of it?' The facility was the busiest airport in Europe – a civil and military mix – literally a flying circus. 'How do they do it?' I wondered. 'And how will I do it?'"

"So, how do they do it?" I asked, imagining the scene Diego was painting, and vowing never again to get on a plane.

"Well, wait, I'll tell you, but there's more. Because the weather was so bad at this airport most of the year, we had a special exception to visual flight rules (VFR), which allowed pilots to fly through clouds without using instruments or radar separation. Most of the traffic was controlled from the tower – *my tower* – not by radar. It was the controller's job – *my job* – to separate the traffic . . . er . . . psychically!"

Well thank goodness for that, I thought, I mean you wouldn't want them to use their eyes or sophisticated instruments when they've got perfectly good psychic powers, now would you?

"The pilot often started off not knowing where he was."

"I don't want to know that, thank you!" I teased, re-affirming my vow to never fly again. "Can we get to the point?"

"This *is* the point! There was a particular moment in that first month of training when I knew that the controllers were controlling air traffic intuitively. That, in fact, that was the primary way they did it.

"For instance, one time a pilot was five seconds overdue on final approach and somehow the controller knew that the pilot had misreported his original position, and didn't really know where he was. The controller made the traffic call based solely on intuition and avoided a mid-air collision just before the plane popped out of the clouds."

"So, what happened when they let you at the controls? Weren't you nicknamed Emergency Mulligan?" I asked with a smile.

"That's true, but I never actually *caused* an emergency; I just happened to be on duty in the Tower when they happened and ended up sorting them out."

I was married to Diego for seventeen years and never *did* quite believe that one.

"Anyway, a few months into my training I was doing it, too – controlling traffic with my intuition! What helped me was knowing it was possible, seeing it with my own eyes and ears every minute of every day and not having an option. I simply *had* to do it! Failure was not an option. Failure meant that planes crashed and people died."

"So, is there a secret way you learned to do this?"

"Not secret, but very specific. You pay attention to the smallest details, like the sound of each different aircraft's microphone turning on or off and the tone of the pilot's voice and breath; whether or not the pilot is excited, anxious, unsure of himself, or relaxed and clear. You practice this until it becomes an impeccable blend of deduction, perception and intuition. Your right and left-brain hemispheres must be working together in total harmony. Of course, I didn't use language like that then – didn't know it existed – but it was what was happening, nonetheless.

"I wish I had an audio recording of those early days, everything I did and everything everyone else did, because it was all recorded, in case we screwed up. The FAA investigation team could dissect the tapes in case of a crash. Talk about accountability! But we were so busy at this tower that sometimes during a shift change in peak traffic you couldn't even brief the controller who was coming to relieve you. Eventually the incoming controller would just tap me on the shoulder and say 'I've got the picture.' And then I'd sign off the log as fast as I could and head for the door."

"OK, so I'm getting the picture, now tell me about one of your famous emergencies," I teased, pouring more tea. "But, remember, I can only include it in the book if there's something intuitive about it."

"No problem – this was definitely intuitive. The first one was during my training. In fact, it was during the emergency landing simulation. Except that it wasn't a simulation – it was a real emergency!

"There was I, in the hot seat on local control talking to planes in the sky within our busy zone, wondering when I would get to work the simulated emergency. My trainer, Klaus, had arranged for the pilot of 18027 to have a mock emergency. So when he called in declaring an emergency, naturally I asked if it was simulated. He responded: ' No, this is an *actual* emergency!' Well, this is a twist I thought, so I quickly polled the ground and flight data controllers next to me: 'Did he say '*actual* emergency?" They nodded affirmatively.

"Trouble was, Klaus heard different. Having set up a fake emergency, his brain seemed unable to hear the word *actual*. Klaus absolutely insisted it was only a simulation. At that moment, my intuition came right in and overrode any doubts. I immediately initiated the crash alarm, just as the pilot confirmed: 'Smoke in the cockpit'. Fighting Klaus, who was by now trying to pull me out of my seat, I cleared the whole control zone, gave the pilot a straight in approach and attempted to get them down before they suffocated.

"The whole time Klaus continued to yell and scream that it was only a simulation and to *not* bring out the fire trucks and to *not* clear central Germany's air space! He was so angry and so certain I was wrong; he had to be physically carried out of the control tower to allow me to do my job. It was not until the plane was on final approach and visibly trailing smoke that poor Klaus believed it was an actual emergency!"

I fell about laughing and Joss, by this time sitting across from his Dad on a stool, was perched on the edge of his seat to hear more.

"Early one morning, I'd just arrived on duty at about 5.45 am and was brewing coffee; it was fairly quiet as the morning rush hadn't yet started. When suddenly I heard: 'Mayday, mayday, mayday,' over the emergency radio frequency. Turned out, a US Air force U-2 spy plane had just been hit by a surface to air missile over East Germany. I stopped making coffee and listened. No one was responding. It seemed that no control tower in all of Europe's air space would answer him, maybe knowing it would consume the rest of their day, if not week, with the search and rescue, mountains of paperwork and intense follow-up investigations. Well, I intuitively decided to answer the distress call – and yes, it did take up the rest of my day! Can't say any more about that one."

"So, you really honed your intuition working all these emergencies?"

"Yes, in fact, we practiced group intuition to deal with lost or downed aircraft. One time, the whole team worked together intuitively. We were all playing cards after the morning rush and I was the only one monitoring the frequencies . . . I should add here that though card playing on duty was never allowed, research proved years later that it keeps people in high-stress jobs alert and on the mental and intuitive edge for action. So, whoever dealt the cards sat out of the game and would cover all the air traffic control tower positions when there was light traffic.

"So, suddenly we all hear a very broken, static-laced transmission: ' ower . . . ive . . . est . . . engine,' followed by a 'chink' sound. That's all we heard and it was gone in a flash. The makeshift card table was instantly kicked over and all four of us totally focussed on the puzzle. We knew the 'chink' was the specific sound of the microphone foot switch on a big CH-47 Chinook helicopter. And we also knew that pilots never mention their engines unless they're not working right! We knew, too, that the static and broken signal meant the aircraft was very low to the ground. No response to our repeated calls meant it was now down. Every fragment of information got factored in and within seconds, using our collective intuition and reasoning powers, we reached consensus on what we'd just heard: A Chinook had just crashed five miles west of our airport.

"We initiated a full-scale search and rescue operation, closed a big portion of German airspace for hours, re-routed a dozen flights, and sent the airport crash crew on a wild treasure hunt – all based mainly on our team intuition. Five miles west of our airport search planes reported nothing unusual, just a farmer burning the stubble off his wheat field. On the surface, that sounded pretty normal for the time of year, but intuitively it didn't. After just a moment's thought, we realised there were no grains growing in that area of Rhineland Pfalz – only grapes. Minutes later, after requesting a closer inspection, the crashed and burning Chinook was spotted in a vineyard. Due to our quick response – and some dumb luck – the whole flight crew survived, despite their cargo of high explosive munitions.

"There's more to this particular story, but I'm saving it for my own book!" Diego concluded. "Plus, I need to be on my way."

Joss was by this time jumping up and down and eager to hear yet another gripping tale. However, we had plans for a movie and Diego had an appointment, so we wound up our chat and said our goodbyes, with Diego promising to tell Joss more stories the following weekend.

The following morning, I was still half asleep when I heard a soft voice call across the hallway: "Hi Mommy…are you awake yet?"

Joss was calling from his room, and on hearing me grunt, which he took for a yes, padded over and clambered into my bed, snuggling up close.

"Hey, there's a book under the pillow and it's lumpy!" He exclaimed.

"I always put books there that I like, or they land there if I fall asleep reading. You should try it when you do a book report at school – saves having to read the whole thing," I teased.

The book was *In Search of The Magic of Findhorn*. Joss read the title and asked "Hey, isn't that the one you and your friend in France wrote?"

"That's right, the advance copy just arrived, and speaking of books, I need to get out of bed in five minutes and finish writing the guidance book."

"What's it going to be called when its finished?"

"*The Findhorn Book of Guidance & Intuition*. Do you know what intuition is?"

"In…tu…ition is like where you just know something but you can't really see it, you just feel it. It's sort of like a kind of déjà vu – sort of," he answered without hesitation. "And deja vu is where you can see into the future, like when you're in a dream and you're talking to your mom about something and then that happens in the day, or like if you just see a bird flying by and then you look away, and then you look again and there's the exact same bird – like you see a few minutes into the future. But really, the future and the past and the present are all happening at the same time; there is no such thing as past or future, there's only the present."

"How do you know that?" I asked incredulously, though at the same time catching the way I fell into an assumption that just because Joss was younger and smaller than me he couldn't know such things. Children have innate wisdom – they just know – they don't have to go to workshops to re-learn what we adults have forgotten.

"Daddy told me," he answered. "We talk about things like that."

"Do you think its true?" I asked.

"Duh!" he exclaimed, in the way children do when pointing out the obvious.

"Mommy, will you write a book about me – totally about me – about my first ten years. I can sit by your computer and tell you things to write. We can call it *The Joss Book* by Carly Newfeld and Joss Mulligan. Khaila can edit it – she writes poetry."

"Well . . ." I began, thinking for a moment.

But Joss soon interjected: "Though, hmmm, when would we have to get it done by?" Seemingly changing his mind at the thought of an imminent deadline.

"Well, you know that book report you have to do by next Thursday… now imagine having a whole book to write by a certain date."

"Do you have to get up and go on your computer?" He asked, sensing my thoughts and snuggling closer.

"Yes, I do, but not for another five minutes," I agreed as he began a playful pillow fight.

"Yeah!" He squealed, "I told you there's only the present."

"And, yes, let's write *our* book," I added. "Though no deadlines, just when we *feel* like writing it!"

"Yeah!" I heard, just as another pillow was hurled towards me.

Chapter 6

BODY OF WISDOM

"Body intuition is the true mind of the body"
[Felix Wolf]

There is an inner voice that is clear and clean. That inner voice is the voice that speaks up for my growth and my integrity. It dares me to go into the unfamiliar amid the voices of fear and protest. You can recognise it because it wants the best for you. That voice wants you to speak up for yourself when you need to, stand up for what you love, walk towards the people that mirror your greatness. It can never be silenced because it is the real you. It tastes like adventure. It's usually accompanied by exhilaration. The body signal is that it gives energy rather than taking energy away.

My friend Maggie Caffery has a way with words that helps me relax and stay with myself rather than search for meaning. Reading her e-mail, I felt a renewed spirit. "You can recognise it because it wants the best for you." Of course! Why on earth would true guidance be trying to trip us up or sabotage us? Even though following guidance may raise obstacles and challenge us to go beyond our petty fears and familiar territory, it is inherently for our good.

The doorbell interrupted my thoughts, and I saw my friend, Allison, standing outside.

"Hey!" We greeted each other with a hug, I put my computer on sleep mode and we headed towards the kitchen and a pot of tea.

"How's the book coming along?" She asked.

"Slow, but fascinating. I've almost finished the interviews and am now piecing it all together, though it's going to be a while yet. Researching and writing this book requires me to be true to my own word, and to pause and breathe and pay attention. I've always been the kind of person who gets intuition on the fly, so to speak, so I am purposefully setting myself more time to meditate and notice how guidance comes to me in other ways, too."

"You have a lot of help, Carly, keep going! I don't mean just practical help; I mean that none of us are alone in this quest. When we pay attention and keep our eyes open we begin to notice how much help we truly have from the unseen worlds.

"One of the things I am remembering," Allison continued, "Is that we have so many resources available – all around us, as well as within. That clear, inner, unmistakable voice is becoming stronger for me, and so are the outer signals. I don't mean the distractions; I mean the outer world signals that show me I am on track. They show up as synchronicities, as marvellous, often laughter-filled moments of 'co-incidence.' As surprises!"

"How do you tell the distractions from the signals?" I asked as we carried our tea out into the garden.

"I notice that when I contract with doubt or worry that my intuition seems to contract, too. I lose my ability to recognise the forms it takes. When I breathe and relax, even for a moment, I seem to get back on track – literally in a groove that seems to lead directly to intuition-land."

We simultaneously laughed at her use of the term "intuition-land." It was not a term I had ever heard her use before.

"It just came out, but it does tell me that there is a place – but I don't think its anywhere we go . . ."

"Or even leave," I added.

"Exactly! It's that eternal, vibrant wellspring: our true centre. All we have to do is notice it and we are there – aligned and sounding our true note within the unified field."

"And, perhaps practice and nourish it, too." I added.

"Yes, nourish it deeply. Nourish – and pay attention."

I agreed: "Attention is the key. Whatever we fix our attention on happens really. So, if our attention is focussed – softly focussed – on staying in our integrity, on speaking the truth, on being the best of ourselves in whatever we're doing and whoever we're with, then we find ourselves staying in the guidance groove . . ."

"And in intuition-land!" Allison reminded me with a smile.

"Well, we've got that figured out. Phew! Glad you came over." I grinned.

After Allison left, inspired by our teatime conversation, I returned to my computer and wrote a letter to a friend in England:

I've just had one of those conversations where the energy spirals higher and higher and where I feel that anything is possible. Although the utter quietness of inner guidance is palpable with the Spirit of God, also speaking about it with a good friend allows me to drop deeper into myself and find hopefulness and active joy.

There are some things I must do soon which require a leap of faith and I now feel that I have a firm enough foundation from which I can take that leap. I've always had that foundation; I just didn't know it before – or I had forgotten it. This may look different for each of us, but it is present. In fact, it is in the present moment – that is exactly where it is – and I can sense it viscerally. I wish I could transmit that to you, because it is so clear to me as I write. Perhaps you can feel through my words this place from where wisdom rises, where peace resides, from where we make clear decisions and take action which is truly joyous, loving, gentle, strong, enfolding, and respectful. We find it the moment we stop striving.

I feel held by God knowing that I live in a benevolent universe, which supports and nourishes me; even though I look around and see and hear the pain and cries in the world, right this moment I feel the immense, sacred and loving world. We do live in a fragile world, we ourselves are fragile and precious in the most wonderful sense of the word and do not truly know what may happen the next moment. So, I am grateful for now, even knowing that this peace may not last. This Spirit is what I will follow without hesitation and let all else fall away.

With love and gratitude, Carly

I finished writing just as the phone rang:

"Hi, Mommy. . . hey, I must tell you . . . !" My seventeen-year-old daughter, Mikhaila, sounded especially happy.

"Where are you?"

"Oh, downtown somewhere, with Katy and Jen and a whole lot of people . . . hey, there's Justin . . ."

The phone went dead and I figured she'd call back moments later.

"Hey, Mom, I'm back, how's the book going?"

"Going well . . . hey, Khaila, can I interview you for it?"

"Sure! What d'you wanna know?"

"Well, first of all, I'd like to know if you get intuitions, I mean I'm pretty sure you do, but we've never really talked about it."

"All the time! I get them all the time, like yesterday, I was on the bus when…hold on a minute, there's another call coming in . . ."

Eventually, Mikhaila and I actually got a chance to talk for ten uninterrupted minutes. How, I wonder, did I ever get through my teens without a cell phone and instant e-mail?

"So, how do you recognise intuition amidst the clamour and all the other voices and distractions?" I asked.

"Easy! I feel it, it's very clear."

"Every time?"

"Pretty much, it's always right on."

"Can you elaborate?"

"Sure, yes, in my stomach – it's a lot like butterflies, like when you're going to meet someone really special – sort of like that, but not quite. That's kind of more exciting. No, if it's a warning type intuition, I feel a knot in my stomach – like I just know, absolutely, that I shouldn't do something or go somewhere. Like one day a whole lot of people were going down to the river . . . and I just got a bad feeling about it in my stomach. Something did happen and I'm really glad I got the feeling and didn't go.

"Sometimes I get signs, too."

"What kind of signs?"

"Oh, you know, like when I see a skateboarder on the Plaza and I just know there's gonna be a cop after him in like three minutes . . . " She laughed.

"Not those kind of signs!" I laughed, too, appreciating her humour. "Are the signs anything specific?"

"No, just random signs. I know them when I see them – but really it's the stomach thing – that's always right.

"Hey, Mommy, I gotta go, I'll let you know if I think of more things, and hey, Mom, I'm about out of contact lenses can you order me some more . . . aw, no, maybe I'll get glasses this time, I'm sick of contacts . . . yes, can we go get glasses – really cool ones?"

And there I was, thinking we'd got through an entire phone call without an expensive request!

"OK, let's talk some more and I'll see what I can do about the glasses." I offered.

"Thanks, Mommy! Later. Love you!"

"Later. Love you, too."

I was reminded how when I was pregnant with Mikhaila I called my unborn child, "my little dolphin," and sure enough, even as a toddler she avidly turned to pages in picture books about dolphins and whales. Now, she advocates for their protection in the world's oceans, and talks about eventually studying marine biology.

∞∞∞

Sunday morning, I had been invited by a new friend, Josefina, to her home in one of the tiny mountain villages of northern New Mexico. From there, we were going up into the hills behind her house to gather medicinal herbs. I arrived a little early, and was pleased to hear that two other people would be joining us a little later. Josefina offered me mint tea and we walked outside together to pick a few handfuls of peppermint and spearmint growing in her garden.

Suddenly she surprised me by saying "I've never really felt completely at home in New Mexico."

I knew she had lived here for many years, after meeting her husband, a New Mexico native, in her own native Bolivia. She talked candidly for a while as she picked the aromatic mints and went back inside to prepare the tea. I asked her if I could tell some of her story in my book and she agreed. "As long as you don't say my name," she added with a wonderful, full laugh – her deep brown eyes twinkling.

"OK, choose yourself a name that I can use."

"My great-grandmother was Josefina, I was seven years old when she passed from this world. I know her spirit lives inside me, especially when I work with the herbs, and I know she's been guiding me my whole life; even though I've made some mistakes, she guides me back on the right road. So, Josefina is the name I would like to use in your book."

I watched her face as she spoke. The high-desert sun had weathered her skin, but it glowed with an inner light of beauty and rare, hard-earned wisdom.

"I came here because I was in love . . . it was like a fairy tale and I let myself get caught in the tale instead of listening inside. I remember the first night we spent alone, without my family nearby, I knew I shouldn't be alone with him, because of what might happen . . ." she giggled, "but you know how these things are.

"I was a good girl, I said 'no' but I saw something in his eyes, something caring and kind and I didn't listen to that 'no.' I knew even that next day I should have. I didn't follow that first intuition. It was not just my religion, my upbringing telling me to say 'no' to this man, it was something else, too. I wanted the warmth he was showing me . . . I let my mind, my feelings, convince me, though I knew inside . . ." she placed her hand just below her belly, "here is where I knew."

The tone of her voice changed as she became suddenly serious and I shivered as if something auspicious was about to happen. Josefina seemed to grow taller right in front of my eyes.

"We were taught as young girls that inside our own bodies is a way to know, inside the womb. It is an empty place, but not empty like nothing; it is full of the potential for life and is like a spring, a well, and the source of the water of life. The witches – the old *brujos* here in the mountains – they know this, the healers, the old midwives – *curanderas* – know this also. The womb is for making babies, but it is also the place of truth and power inside. It is not passive, waiting to be filled, it is full already, and you decide how you want to use it."

I glanced around Josefina's simple kitchen, with its uneven brick floor, shelves lined with dozens of jars of fruits, jams and honey; strings of herbs hanging to dry from the wood-lined ceiling, and braids of garlic by the door. Our tea was ready and we sat at the table in the centre of the room. Seconds after I sat down a large, sleek cat jumped in my lap. I stroked it with respect.

"I learned to store power in my womb, I learned that when I wanted to know something or to do something big, that I first had to put that seed of a thought – that intuition, however small – into the womb and let it grow in there. The *curanderas* say that is where we store intent, and it is the womb that guides us if we let it. This . . . secret . . ." Josefina hesitated a moment, as if she wasn't sure she should be telling me all this. "This is told to us girls when we are young. Our brothers are not so lucky; they have to use their minds to figure things out, but we can go straight to our womb." She laughed and got up to fetch a jar of honey from one of the rather rickety-looking shelves. I wasn't quite sure if I was in Pooh Bear's house in the Hundred Acre Wood or an Andean village in South America! Josefina seemed to pick up on my unspoken thought.

"Even as we are speaking about this, we find ourselves using the power in our wombs. Even though you didn't know this before now, it was always there for you. Now you know . . ." She hesitated again and closed her eyes. "Now you know this, you won't easily forget it. Put this knowledge – these words – in your womb, though you might not understand all what I'm saying."

"Can I put this in my book?"

This time she didn't hesitate: "Yes. This world, now, the way it is, especially here in North America, we need to know this about ourselves. Put it in your book, Carly. I will tell you more I want you to write about it."

Her last sentence was more a demand than a comment. It came from her womb and I knew it. She didn't smile when she said it, this time her soft eyes held strictness, a flash of fire I had not seen before. I knew I would write more, but first I had to learn and experience for myself the power and secrets held in my own womb and even as I thought it, I sensed it was something that could take years of practice; something I had to take very seriously.

"The power you feel," Josefina again observed my thoughts, "this powerful strength is the intent of the womb. And so is the special quietness you can feel now."

I hadn't noticed till that moment how still everything had become; even the bees a few yards away in their hive by the orchard seemed to have hushed their buzzing. The kitty had climbed off my lap and was curled up asleep on a pile of blankets.

"This quiet is also from the womb. The womb is mysterious, Carly, it is both the source of what we call 'intent' and also the source of dreaming – what you would call perhaps daydreaming – when you let yourself float a little, when you let the mind pause its constant chattering. Listen to your daydreaming as well as to your night time dreams. Your dreaming mind has information for you, too. Pay attention to it, but soften your eyes . . . your inward gaze . . . as you do."

"Kind of like in meditation?" I asked.

"I do not meditate, not in the way you have learned here." She was speaking softly, as if not to disturb the silence with words.

"It is not emptying the mind, it is not focus or . . ." She searched for words and I sensed her search was not so much because she was looking for the words in English, but for any words that truly described the mystery of the womb.

"We are dreaming now, together." She said this in almost a whisper, close to my ear so I could feel her breath on my face. "Soften your gaze, do not try to concentrate. You will 'see' what is just beyond your vision, around the edges, blurry. But you do not need to look for it. Feel it. Feel it. Yes, like that . . ."

Perhaps it was Josefina's presence that touched mine, as I felt myself dropping into a place inside, or outside – I couldn't tell and it didn't matter.

It wasn't my mind either, even though I noticed thoughts, they did not seem to come from the usual part of me. And neither were they what others have described as "the still, small voice." My whole body seemed to be floating and belonged to the house and the house belonged to outside. I felt a deep peace and at the same time an extraordinary clarity. I felt as if I had expanded and grown bigger; there felt to be no separation between my physical body and the things around me, especially the natural things, the water, trees, and the hills in the distance.

For a split second I thought I was standing on a hill, which I knew was several miles away. I also sensed – and here it is hard for me to find words to describe – that my memory belonged to millions of memories, all my own, all in every cell of my body; that I had recorded inside me the history of the ancient world and whenever I needed to know something, I could just know it. The past, the present, and the future were all one and yet were not anything; they were at once immense infinity and yet completely of no consequence. And woven through all the images was an all-pervading love, that was both powerful – bringing tears to my eyes – and also utterly impersonal.

I heard a clap – or something like a clap – and suddenly I was back in Josefina's kitchen in my very solid, normal state of consciousness. She looked at me with kind eyes and smiled. Again, I had the distinct impression that she knew everything I had just experienced.

"Yes, I helped you a little bit, but you did that mostly by yourself. You have power, Carly. You might want to call it an 'out of the body' experience, but it is going into the body, not out. It is not what others call 'psychic,' it is . . ." Again, she hesitated, seeming to search for words. "All humans have this 'other' place within them. All. It is essential to our very survival. It is easier . . . natural, for women because we have a womb and can store the energy and memory there. Men, they can go there when they learn to discipline the mind, open the heart, and love. It is what men are looking for in a woman. The power attracts. All female animals store power in their womb. When two males fight over a female, it is the power in the female's womb they want. They sense it."

The direction of the conversation was turning into an area I had wondered about since she first began speaking.

"So, what happens when we actually use our wombs to have babies, and even, well, you did bring it up earlier…have sex?" I wasn't at all sure whether Josefina would want to answer this.

"This is the book I want you to write one day, or maybe I will write it and you will help me!" Her eyes flashed again. "Suffice to say, now, that we also have the power and skills to purify and rebuild our womb – just like any part of the body. This is the healer's part, but it is also our part; we do it with our thoughts and our breath, remembering everything and letting it go with the breath."

She turned her head to one side, breathing slowly in as she did so, and turning her head to the other side, blew out that breath as if blowing out birthday candles. She nodded in my direction, instructing me to do the same.

"Think of something, perhaps something that disturbed you, maybe words someone said to you that hurt. See the person, hear the words as you breath in and now turn your head to the right and blow out the hurt."

Closing my eyes I did as she told me. Seconds later, I opened them wide.

"Whoa!" I exclaimed, "I'd been carrying that around with me all weekend and now it's gone! I can feel it, as if it left my body, not just my mind."

We both turned in the direction of the sound of a pick-up truck turning onto the gravel driveway, still a hundred yards from the front door.

"I must ask you one more question," I said quickly, wishing I had time for many more.

"You said at the beginning you didn't really feel quite at home here, but you are here, and you say you are guided in your life by the spirit of your great-grandmother, and your inner knowing. Have you not been guided to leave?"

Josefina looked directly at me; this time her eyes were neither soft nor flashing fire and I sensed sadness, but I wasn't sure if that's what I really saw.

"I will know when to leave. I love this land, especially the beauty of the land and the people here, and I love my husband dearly. There have been, and still are, lessons for me to learn here. I cannot go back to that first moment when I 'should' have said 'no' and didn't. So, that day, my life took a different direction, a different turn, and I followed it. It would be a waste of energy to regret or be resentful or beat my own self up for doing something wrong, or even judging it was wrong. The breathing I showed you, it is a way of restoring energy and recapitulating the past, taking what we might call mistakes and reusing the energy, restoring our own power circuits . . . and . . ."

A light knock on the door interrupted us and a petite woman wearing a funky blue hat popped her head around the doorway. Seconds later a frisky, black puppy bounded into the kitchen, quickly followed by a second woman who tried to round her up, but by this time the pup was running excitedly in circles around Josefina's kitchen. The cat fled!

The woman with the hat was introduced to me as Beth-Ann and the owner of the lively puppy as Deborah. Josefina put cups of steaming tea on the table and Deborah sat on the floor with the puppy, calming her down with light touches behind the ears. Josefina and her husband own a German Shepherd with a Wolf forefather; he was away for the weekend on a trip with her husband. The pup could undoubtedly smell Wolf.

The rest of the day was spent hiking up in the hills, with Josefina showing us numerous plants and talking about their history in this area, their medicinal properties and how she would later prepare and store them. We carried baskets as well as backpacks, gathering some herbs, leaving others. We were out till early evening, leaving me with a few hours of daylight left to drive home safely on the twisty, turning lanes. Josefina invited me to come back some day and I gratefully accepted her invitation.

∞∞∞

A few days later I was getting ready for a party at a friend's ranch a few miles outside town; I took a shower, washed my hair, and laid out my yoga blanket in a shady spot on the back patio to do a few stretches before finally getting changed and leaving for the evening.

I didn't have time to do a full set of postures, so instead did a few warm ups and followed where my body wanted to go. I stretched my fingertips to the blue sky, yawning as I did so, naturally releasing built up tension and feeling the joy and freedom of my body's ability to stretch luxuriously and then relax completely.

I turned to face the setting sun in the west and moved effortlessly into a series of Salute to the Sun postures, keeping my eyes open to watch the colours merging from azure to turquoise, to amber to coral. A swathe of radiant gold seemed to fill the entire western sky.

I lay on my back, arms outstretched, and as I did so random thoughts – like birds flying across the clear sky – scudded across my mind. Tears welled in my eyes as I noticed the surfacing thoughts, which came into focus and then released with the tears and sighs that came naturally through my breath.

After about ten minutes of this sweet stillness I became aware that so much of my own ability to access intuition and inner guidance comes from this daily practice; this time I give to myself, no matter what else is calling me in my life. I awake around six most mornings just to have this time for myself before my son wakes up, or my daughter calls, and we all begin the busyness of the day. I take time to meditate, even if its only five minutes, and I also choose an active meditation like yoga or martial art type movements, which allow my body to re-integrate and restore its equilibrium.

Over the years, I have noticed how much I store in my body – not just tension and stress and toxins – but thoughts which seem to get stuck in my very joints or just below the surface of my skin. I dry brush before my morning shower; a habit I picked up from a Finnish flatmate in London years earlier. The brushing, breathing and stretching are all ways I keep my physical body alert, flexible and open to the ever-flowing changes of daily life. I also drink lots of water (essential when living in the high desert of New Mexico!) and pay attention to what I put onto my body – not just in my mouth.

Instead of heavily scented and sticky body lotions, I use only cold-pressed sesame oil and add my own favourite essential oil – usually rose or sandalwood. I massage it on my arms and legs when my pores are still open from a warm bath or shower, letting the fragrant sesame sink slowly into my skin and the natural vitamins in the oil nourish me.

Our bodies provide an extraordinary palate of inner guidance if we treat them lovingly and pay attention to what they have to tell us.

Later that evening, at the party, I listened in to a conversation between my friends Ed and Robert on the subject of body intuition and using muscle testing as a way to confirm intuition. They were well into a conversation about dowsing when I arrived.

"Now dowsing, as I understand it," Robert was saying, "is a method for discovery based on intuition. The dowsing rod or the pendulum is nothing more than an amplifier of intuitive knowledge, to the point that it can be consciously registered. If you see it that way, then how does muscle testing fit in? When I was introduced to kinesiology I remained sceptical, as I experienced no muscle weakening when we paired off and tried it. Whose intuition is being tapped, I wondered, the tester's or the testee's?"

"Brilliant, very good question!" Ed exclaimed. "Frankly, it may be neither, or it could be both, or it could be one or the other. Since it's an energetic transfer of information, it could come from some 'higher intelligence' that has been expressly or unintentionally invoked to help sort things out. Really clear muscle responses, which either 'lock' or 'limp', more often than not derive from the testee's body manager . . ."

"That's a great term – body manager." Robert interrupted.

"Yes, I first heard it from a wonderful elder called Sara Marriott in the Findhorn Community back in the seventies and I've used it ever since. As a practitioner of kinesiology for many years, to keep my intuition and/or bias from interfering, I set the intent by telling my client, 'We're going to talk to your Body Manager.' If or when I slip over into my own intuition I tend to notice how the muscle response is more tentative, not as clear; so I reset the intent. It's possible that the more tentative test results arise when I or someone else has biases or worldviews that somehow conflict with the testee's or their healing angels. That said, the less clear or ambiguous responses may be due to the fact that the statement one makes, or the question asked, is out of timing or out of sync with the priorities of the body manager. There is a way of prioritising using finger modes that makes eminent sense, but it is not taught usually in beginners' classes.

"My guess, Rob, is that when you were first introduced to muscle testing, your muscles stayed locked when someone 'tested' you. This always happens to someone when they have their 'critical/analytical switch' in the 'on' position. Some never turn it off for long enough to experience the 'test' kinaesthetically. It's a challenging scenario for any practitioner, but the more experienced practitioners know how to deal with it. I have several ways to calm the anxious testee, but one should never attempt to force one's way through the 'on' switch. That may cause physical harm as well as intellectual and emotional insult. It is clear that sometimes all of us want our conscious mind to be in control, to assess everything with reason and logic. The body doesn't work that way, nor does the body manager."

Robert was nodding thoughtfully.

"One last thing. Look at it this way: Some subtle intelligence (I happen to call it the body manager) breathes us, digests our food, identifies and distributes nutrients, regulates temperature, acid-alkaline balance, and tells us when to pee and a host of other things – seamlessly. If we tried to do that with our conscious minds we would be out of business in seconds!"

The two men laughed heartily.

"So, on we go into the ultimate wonder and mystery of it all!" I heard Robert conclude, as he and Ed wandered into the next room to meet others in the crowd and search out the table covered with yummy goodies such as lasagne, fresh-baked breads, and an array of delicious salads.

Me? I headed for the guacamole and chips, poured myself a sparkling water with a little red wine and went across to the nearby barn where a marimba band was setting up to play a gig. Then I danced till I dropped sometime early the next morning.

Chapter 7

Maps and Guides – and the Voices of Children

"I have my ancestral teachers and the Stone People who tell me the 'stories' of what has happened in places. I relax, breathe, turn inwards, open my inner vision and there they are!"

[Amantha Murphy]

I live in the American Southwest, where observing signs from nature is inherent to the native, indigenous people. A friend of mine, who grew up in northern New Mexico among *curanderas* and traditional craftspeople, told me how throughout her childhood, being in rhythm with the wheel of the year and the turning of the seasons was "just the way life was." She didn't think of it as magic.

She explained: "There were good years and seasons of bounty and plenty, and there were times when the rains didn't come and the *acequias* (irrigation ditches) ran dry. We always had enough food stored, but we would pray and dance and make special offerings to the Spirits of the Land in the special places."

New Mexico has always drawn people looking for that "magic" and searching for spiritual direction from the local Indian peoples; and more recently to learn the innovative ways of the new teachers who bridge spiritual growth, psychology, science, and healing. My friend was truly blessed to learn from her family about the wisdom of the earth. Many of us are raised without such simple nourishment and guidance from "Grandmother Earth and Grandfather Sky."

Although the primary purpose of this book is to direct the reader inward to their wellspring of guidance, it would not be complete without a brief look at the way signs from nature, symbols and maps of every kind serve us. I will do my best here to present a few which I have personally experienced and which I have used over the years to confirm my own inner guidance.

As I explored many techniques and systems of "outer" guidance for this book, I frequently heard stories where outer guidance and interior self appeared to seamlessly merge. At first, I didn't think I would include them – intent as I was on retaining the "purity" of discovering only inner authority! Like many writers, however, I learned to put aside my own judgments and propensity to categorise and saw how guidance manifests in myriad forms, each perfect for the person who needs it at that moment. This was especially so when I saw how the words and examples of inner spiritual teachers touched the lives of so many.

Amantha lives in a small village on the west coast of Ireland. We met in London in the early 80's and have remained friends across the miles. I deeply respect her wisdom, culled from her Celtic roots and honed through raising four children. More recently, as her children grew, she returned to counselling others using her attunement to the ancient Goddess energy of her native Ireland.

"I've had my guidance with me for as long as I remember," Amantha told me.

"It was only as I grew older that I realised others did not have that inner voice as I did. The guidance is there constantly, like the very air I breathe. When I hear the voice of guidance all other voices seem empty. There is always a sense of rightness with the guidance; a sense of knowing, of clarity, as if time has stopped for that moment. I feel it from the centre of my body outwards.

My primary guide is my spiritual teacher who I call 'The Lady' as well as the living forces around me, especially the 'Stone People' and the elements of Air, Fire and Water."

"The Stone People?" I asked.

"The stones are our cousins, they hold the stories and the energy of the land in balance and they 'sing' the song of the earth. It is this song that keeps the land in balance with itself. People removing the large stones and bombarding stones with ultrasound so they may use them unbalances the land, and therefore the people. We are connected; our bones are like the stones. The Stone People are not heavy or dull, but bright and light. Each stone has its own character and can be held often for grounding and connecting. The world is alive within every atom and everything upon the earth holds the song – the dream. We have forgotten that dream but they sing it to us constantly to remind us."

Amantha's words brought to mind for me the "song lines" of the Aboriginal people, and also of the mysterious migratory patterns of birds; patterns even today not completely understood by science. As she spoke, images of nomadic people from around the globe flashed through my consciousness, and a memory – possibly a collective memory – of rites such as throwing of the bones and the reading of runes surfaced momentarily.

"So, guidance comes to me in many different ways," Amantha continued. "The Lady, an inner voice, flashes of intuition, signs from nature – such as seeing a certain bird or animal – my inner knowing self, dreams, angels. It comes especially when there is a need from another, it just manifests as the words or actions through me."

I asked Amantha if she could give me an example.

"Yes, my guidance told one mother here in Ireland to tell her daughter to leave her work before September 2001. This was in April and her daughter worked in one of the twin towers in New York City. Another example is concerning a woman who was planning on taking her own life. My guidance told her how and even when she was planning it, and helped her to understand what was happening to her and how to move on with her life in a different way.

"Often guidance helps those 'stuck' on their path. I have always trusted my guidance; it is the one sense I always have complete faith in."

"Do you make a distinction between guidance and intuition?" I asked.

"I've been working in this sphere for many years and I would say that they seem to be one. Recognising separation is an illusion. Also, I feel myself growing into my teacher, The Lady. She has been present with me for so long now that I am slowly dropping away the barriers to 'pure experience,' which allows me to be present for her expression to come through me. As well as The Lady, I have my ancestral teachers and the Stone People who tell me the stories of what has happened in places. I relax, breathe, turn inwards, open my inner vision and there they are!"

∞∞∞

Since ancient times and in all cultures, maps, symbols and signs have been used to either confirm guidance or point the way beyond the conflicts or intricacies of the human mind. One of the most well known of all the maps is astrology. The oldest evidence of astrological study is found within China, where the ancient Chinese meticulously preserved their astrological records. Two thousand years before Christ, the Chinese accurately determined the length of the year and also mapped the paths of the sun and moon clearly enough to predict eclipses. Astrologers and astronomers worked hand-in-hand for millennia in India, Mesopotamia, Chaldea, and Babylonia, and for centuries in Europe astrology was courted and respected.

My twin sister, Sarah, has been an astrologer for over 25 years and I asked her why – if we have everything we need inside – do we still need outer maps? And whether astrology replaces or enhances her natural intuition?

"It confirms and enhances," she explained, "I would never say it replaced my intuition, though it does gives me a way of seeing a bigger picture. I may decide something intuitively and might then look at the chart for that day – or a week later. In retrospect, I realise that was the perfect day to do what I had to do. Other times, I may just look at certain aspects and get an intuitive hit; I don't necessarily need to look at the entire chart. The truth is not in the chart, it is inside, but the chart may reflect and confirm what I am sensing.

"After 25 years practicing astrology I still have reverence and awe for the power, energy and mystery of the cosmos. I have enormous respect for the practice of astrology – and ultimately go to the God within. That is the difference between fate and free will. I don't use astrology to give me 'yes' and 'no' answers, but use it in synergy with inner guidance and to support what I feel is right."

Ancient Judaic texts show the relationship between astrology and the Kabbalah. *The Sepher Yetzirah* – a Kabbalistic source translated into English as *The Book of Creation* by Aryeh Kaplan – suggests that Abraham gifted this text to his children and that it connects the mysticism of the Hebrew alphabet with the signs of the zodiac. *The Sepher Yetzirah*, along with *The Zohar*, is a primary source for the Kabbalah. The Hebrew Kabbalah is said to reveal the complete esoteric teachings that have been received by humans from the spirit world, including the mystery of written symbol and numerology, the lore and hierarchy of the Angelic World, dream symbolism, sacred geometry, and also the Tree-of-Life.

Perhaps the most well known ancient book of divination is *The I'Ching – The Book of Changes*, which has been practiced in China for thousands of years. The *I'Ching* is considered a common source for both Confucianism and Taoism and appears to be one of humanity's earliest examples of understanding and conveying the inter-relationship between the human psyche and the universe, the microcosm and the macrocosm. The Yin-Yang principle inherent within the *I'Ching* represents the constant change and motion of the universe and thus of human experience.

∞∞∞

"We, as a species, as well as the spiritual hierarchy, are evolving. At crucial transitions in our evolution we receive assistance from guides who are so good at leading that most of the time we don't know they are there."

[Genoa Bliven]

I have recently been introduced to the Human Design System (HDS), a synthesis of the *I'Ching*, Astrology, the Kabbalah, and the Hindu Chakra system. When I first heard the name I had one of those clear "ah-ha" moments, alerting me to some significance that it held for my life. I have come to trust my own "ah-ha's" well enough to pay attention and to find out more. So, I asked my friend Genoa how the Human Design System harmonised with our innate intelligence and intuition – if, in fact, it did. I wanted to know if maps like HDS and astrology, and oracles like the *I'Ching* or Tarot, replaced our intuition, or whether in some way they supported and accelerated the process. It turned out that this very question was at the heart of Genoa's own investigation into HDS and his story is worth telling:

"There was someone in my community who had studied early on with the person to whom the Human Design System was revealed. Her name was Yola and she kept telling me that I needed to come and see her; she had been given my birth time from a mutual friend and had done my chart! Seeing my design, she was convinced she absolutely had to speak to me about HDS; she saw that I would be integral to the development of the knowledge.

"At that point, I had been an astrologer doing 'intuitive astrology' readings for about twenty years. I was using normal Western astrological techniques and because the information I was getting from that system was very open and sometimes general, I was largely using my intuitive powers to do readings."

"How did you do that?" I interjected. "Be specific," I added.

"A person would come to me for a reading and while in meditation together I would ask them to say their name aloud. By listening to the intonation of their voice I would see their whole life and their attitude towards living. I used my knowledge of astrology to structure what I then told them.

Hearing their name was a way of priming the pump, so to speak. Once the flow began I would hear information transmitted to me from just behind and above my right ear. I considered myself to be a translator. I would be told information about this person and their life and purpose in a language that I described as essence and feeling. I would then translate this into English. Astrology helped me to verify what I was hearing. In fact, this is how I really learned advanced astrology, not from a book, but from an intuitive voice.

"So, when Yola kept telling me that I *must* come to see her, I kept putting her off. I was, after all, doing just fine with the method I used. I was also raising a family of four children and running a manufacturing business. Eventually, however – I'm not sure quite how – I ended up over at her house one day. She welcomed me in and over tea began reading my HDS chart. As she spoke, however, something very significant happened: I was an experienced astrologer who by that time and had read over 5,000 charts, I was aware of the mistakes that other astrologers generally made when they looked at my chart *and she didn't make any of them*!

"You better believe I sat up and paid attention as she went on to do a reading, which spoke about my life in a way that I had only recently come to understand myself. She showed me how it was part of my design to manifest so much activity in my life, and to take so much responsibility – which was still a total surprise to me. An hour later, when she said goodbye, she handed me a bunch of books and said, 'Study these.' I immediately began to do HDS charts for my friends and family and particularly comparison charts for people close to me, including my wife of many years. I immediately saw the issues that had evolved in our relationship right in front of me, printed in black and white. Then, looking at my own chart, I began to learn things about myself; things I realised I would have had to live to 300 years of age to recognise.

"So, Genoa," I interrupted, "how does a map like HDS blend with the intuition of the client? How do we – any of us – find a balance between our own guidance and that revealed by a chart? That's what I *really* want to know?"

"A very good question, and I'm coming to it! My own story ultimately answered exactly that," he grinned. "A little bit more?"

I nodded my okay. I knew Genoa enough to know that he didn't waste words. He was in a flow, and I'd better pay attention.

"So, here I am," he continued, "I've been doing intuitive readings for twenty-something years, relying upon intuition to pull all kinds of info into the world for other people, and now here I am coming into contact with an extraordinarily intricate system which placed the same kinds of intuitive knowing right before me, mapped out in a complex system of undeniable integrity. As you know, the Human Design System was received in eight days and nights of transmission in 1987. I realised over time that nobody could have actually thought this up! It was a revelation, not something contrived.

"At first, I had considerable trouble believing or just 'getting' that major revelations come into the human community from the spiritual planes in such a detailed form. What I had in front of me was something that was not only a result of contact with a super-conscious entity, but also a revelation, which was exact down to the decimal place, as exact as the genetic code itself. For me, it was the first practical contact with something that was so clearly a revelation. I was having an experience of seeing my own intuition superseded."

"That raises a huge issue," I interrupted again, "here I am, in chapter seven of the book already and you've just turned my entire premise on its head!"

"You bet!" He grinned again, and motioned me to continue listening.

"At that same time, I had just finished a training in Hypnotherapeutic Healing and I was convinced that a person's own process must reign supreme for healing to be productive, but here I was confronted with something so extraordinary I knew I had to learn it."

"So, how did you resolve it?"

"What ensued was a year and a half of internal struggle, where I was attempting to understand how this system was put together; studying the *I'Ching*, the Chakra System and the Kabbalah in their relation to astrology and using all the intuition I had at my disposal. In fact, such inquiry on my part was exactly what Yola had in mind. She gave me the books and died three months later."

We were both silent for a moment.

"Yola had felt that based upon my design I had the capability to crack the system; to find out the core of this revelation and how it was internally mathematically consistent. But, what I found as I delved deeper and deeper into the system was that the science did not exist in the world to track the fusion of systems – the *I'Ching*, Kaballah, the Chakra system and Astrology – that had occurred on a higher plane of consciousness. This fusion had occurred on a level of consciousness that went *beyond* my own intuition."

"I can taste this vibration as we speak," I said, sensing the field around us subtly shifting, the veils between worlds thinning. I noticed how alert and awake I was, and how open, soft and receptive.

"Intuition as I understand it – and as I am writing about it in this book – stems from the unified field of consciousness that we can access. So what field were you attuning to that is *beyond* even what we call the unified field?"

"Carly, there were times when I would have the experience of seeing the point of synthesis of these systems – which are very specific and exact – literally disappear into the light! So, there's this simply amazing experience of realising that the spiritual planes which stretch on and on through a spiritual hierarchy are specific to those Beings which inhabit that hierarchy; but that we as human beings – if I'm any example – are being given something through HDS that reveals our potential to relate to each other in an extraordinarily specific way, a way we are generally unconscious of. It is like a technology of the future. And yet it has come into the world for a very specific reason."

"Well, Genoa, we've got this far, so I hope you're about to tell me that reason?" I teased. We both laughed.

"We, as a species, as well as the spiritual hierarchy, are evolving. At crucial transitions in our evolution we receive assistance from guides who are so good at leading that most of the time we don't know they are there. Amongst other things, HDS shows that we are coming up to a point where there will be a mutation in the human species; we are approaching a time when we will become emotionally aware and be able to co-operate with each other in ways that presently we can only dream of. The HDS came into the world in order to assist people to be energetically aware of how they interact with others. The goal of the system is not to understand oneself intellectually, or even intuitively, but rather to convey a method through which we can stop trying to be all things to all people.

"The reason for this work is that the children of the future, who will have capabilities which far outshine ours, will need to be greeted and educated by people who know how to inhabit their bodies and function in an exact way in the world.

"What the HDS maps, is the mystery of how we come into the world needing to have experience. What we generally do is to identify with the experience, rather than allowing ourselves to simply have it."

I sighed a sigh of knowing when Genoa said that, recognising how constantly I was on my own case, always striving instead of accepting.

"Our experience is inconsistent. That is the nature of being in a body. When we agreed to incarnate we agreed to live within limitation so that we can have experience. Through the guidance of HDS we allow other people to play their parts and discover unity. To play our part, we allow other people to play their parts and thus communicate and discover unity by a different path. We can let people be. We can let ourselves be.

"This gives us the opportunity to assist in the birthing of a new consciousness. We are on the threshold of a global emotional intelligence where we will be able to be in relationship, and be aware of what is happening in that relationship at the same time. The children of the future will be able to cooperate in ways beyond our imagination, but they need energetically aware parents and educators.

"Only recently, I have begun to work directly with the intuition of my clients in trance, guiding them to discover their amazing human design and high-functioning reality for themselves, while I use their charts to guide them in the process. This work deeply inspires me; I can feel the future radiating through it."

We didn't need any more words; we just sat quietly together for a while, sipping our tea.

∞∞∞

"Do you remember what that message is?
'You are already enlightened . . . you already have everything you need
to be happy and create a world of peace.'"

[Thomas, a child in Bulgaria]

Genoa's vision of the children of the future is already at hand. James Twyman is the author of *Emissary of Love: The Psychic Children Speak to the World*, a true account of his meeting with and learning from four psychic children who were being trained at a monastery in Bulgaria. James travels the world as an emissary of peace and love, most especially to countries torn and ravaged by war. At the time of writing (early October, 2002) James is travelling to Iraq to focus a worldwide prayer vigil to promote a peaceful solution to the conflict between Iraq and the USA. In a letter, James wrote:

Together we are called to recognise that there is a force more powerful than our military weapons. It is the force of prayer, and I believe that it is the most powerful force in the universe.

In the early summer of 2002, completely unexpectedly, James began receiving messages from one of the children he met in Eastern Europe, a young boy named Thomas.

The following is an excerpt James forwarded from one of Thomas's messages. It speaks for itself of the simplicity of truth:

The Children want to deliver their messages of peace and hope more directly than ever before. Many of you have felt their influence upon your mind and heart, and you know that we have been reaching out to you. But this next stage requires a Community of people who stand beside the Children, focusing their energy more profoundly than ever before. We see gatherings taking place that will increase the momentum we are all feeling. The Psychic Children will deliver their messages at these gatherings, and you will feel the Truth in your souls. This will create a world movement of peace, radiating out from this Community and touching every person now alive. You are being called to be part of that movement. Will you respond?

These gatherings will be our chance to extend and develop the Psychic Children's message. Do you remember what that message is? 'You are already enlightened . . . you already have everything you need to be happy and create a world of peace.' Miracles will occur when you come together in this way, and they will show the world that the shift we are describing is real. Don't be fooled by the darkness that seems to envelope the world right now. Everything is happening exactly as it should. And remember, the time has arrived when innocence will prevail, when the Children will lead the way into the Light.

Peace, James Twyman

Reading Thomas's letter to James, I am reminded that His Holiness the Dalai Lama once said that true peace will come to the world when the children are respected and truly heard. It seems that the words of Thomas, and children all over the world, must be heard and perhaps they are some of the few voices outside our own inner voice that we must pay attention to.

My friend Bruce had a dream two months before his son, who is now eight, was born. In the dream, he heard a voice saying: "I'm not coming into this world to entertain or be cute for anyone. My size will deceive those who need to be . . . see me fully and you will be free." Bruce awoke from the dream understanding that children are born whole, fully receptive and aware, and that to consciously practice seeing his child "fully" meant he had to unravel all the beliefs he carried about children and about being a parent. Years later, he realised that what appeared as the fragile-ness of his newborn son, was not the child's, it was his own, his own innocence manifesting in front of his eyes.

When we feel our own innocence, reflected in the eyes of children, then perhaps we will have no more need for maps and guides.

Chapter 8

EVERYDAY PRESCIENCE

"There is a sweet taste to clear guidance or intuition. . . like fruit nectar. I feel a whole-being resonance that signals to me this is something to pay attention to. When I ignore it, things generally don't go well! I've learned to listen closely and take appropriate action."

[Shari Mueller]

Like many writers, I take a notebook everywhere I go – sometimes even to the movies. I sit in the dark and scribble between bites of popcorn. Not soppy words or clever wit from the screen, but my own thoughts inspired by the energy of the movie; the amplified tone of the emotion, the breadth of colour and landscape. When I'm in a writing mood, everything and anything becomes a possibility for a plot, a line, even a word.

On Saturday mornings I head to the Farmers' Market, find a comfortable straw bale to sit on near the burrito and coffee stand and watch the relaxed and colourful faces jostling in the crowd. The youth marimba band plays at one end of the market and the Suzuki violinists fiddle at the other – amidst goat cheese purveyors, herbalists, and Jake's sweet corn.

There's always an old, green truck in the parking lot plastered with bumper stickers and one in particular always catches my attention, it reads:

"Don't believe everything you think!" I get a distinct "ah-ha" every time I see it and wonder where I can get one from to put on my car (I wonder if it comes as a refrigerator magnet, too?). As I let my imagination fly, I change the words around in my head to "Don't believe *anything* you think!" But, what if what I'm thinking is a useful and helpful thought, like the ones I'm putting into words now?

After several Saturday's musing this atop my straw bale, I had another realisation: "Think" wasn't the key word on the bumper sticker, nor was "anything" or "everything" – it was *believe*! With a stunning flash that rippled down my spine like the hot burrito I was munching, I realised the brilliance of the phrase, "Whatever we *believe* controls our thinking and ultimately denotes what happens!" Beliefs run our lives, beliefs good-naturedly laid down by our parents during our childhoods, judiciously taught in school, and carefully canned by advertisers. All these beliefs we've swallowed over the years and internalised as our own. And most of the time they're not ours!

Test this out any time – I often find myself doing it. I can be speaking on the phone with a friend when I hear myself make a comment on something my friend just said: I might be agreeing with her, I might not, that's not the point. In my voice I hear a tone that isn't quite real, that isn't really "mine." I actually feel it in the back of my throat. My comment to my friend has a deadness about it, a slightly repetitive tone, a trace of something. When I catch myself doing this, I stop. I pause. I might even say, "Oh, that's not what I mean." I don't apologise because apology is over used and most of the time carries the same unbelievable tone, unless it comes from the heart. The heart is where real words, real knowing originates.

So, how on earth *do* I hold normal, everyday conversations without being over critical and madly watchful? I don't. Well, there I catch myself lying again; I'm not quite there yet! However, I am learning to stay inside the quiet place in my heart, to speak less and listen more, to put down the phone earlier, and to move away from the small talk in the market before I'm full. It's subtle. It's not impolite and I do still have many close friends and lots of acquaintances; I just notice how sometimes I unnecessarily add to the cacophony of white noise chatter in the world, or to the idle gossip which perpetuates the veneer of beliefs. I don't want to do that.

This awareness of conversation, small talk, and pleasant idle chatter is just that – awareness. However, noticing it around you, and *choosing* whether or not to participate in any given moment is part of the practice of listening deeper and ultimately making space for the quieter voices of intuition and guidance. Such inner spaciousness is what attracts us to people who we sense "run deep" or who appear to us as wise, thoughtful and insightful; people whose internal dialogue – the chattering mind – is less active, whose brain waves are more balanced between alpha and beta. What appears to be their thoughtfulness is, in fact, the opposite, their minds are quieter and thoughts less cluttered. We sense it.

Often, though, what might start out as "small talk" soon becomes big talk, or something more. Back to the Saturday morning farmers' market again, because it's one of those places where this happens a lot. Maybe it's the atmosphere, the fresh air, or the relaxed unhurried pace; maybe it's the colours, smells and sounds that combine to give it a special flavour and ambiance, I don't know. It's just market day in town, and people can let down their guard.

First stop was by my favourite herbalist's booth to pick up a jar of freshly made lavender face cream. Mmm, the scent of lavender oil with a touch of frankincense sent my olfactory senses deliciously reeling as my desert-parched skin soaked up the aromatic lotion. I went on to fill my canvas tote bag to overflowing with fresh veggies, a wild-crafted, herbal tincture for chamisa pollen allergies, and an armful of glorious flowers.

I headed over to the straw bales for a rest and barely noticed a light tap on my shoulder, so occupied was I jotting down some notes. My good friend James had spotted me from a distance and had come over to say hello.

"What you doin'?" he asked, between bites of apricot turnover.

"Just taking notes for my next book, it's about guidance and intuition."

"Oh, really!" He exclaimed, "that's so funny – well really, it's not – I've been having a seemingly exponential increase in synchronicities and keep getting signs, hearing the same words over and over again, things like that."

He offered me the other turnover, which he'd bought for someone else. I felt I should politely decline, but he insisted.

"So, what do you think it means?" I asked, flaky pastry pieces scattering all over my skirt as I bit into the delicious, straight-from-the-oven treat (James said the baker told him the apricots were picked last night and the turnovers baked that morning).

"I've noticed that if something impresses me, a symbol, maybe a dream, or something that keeps repeating, it strikes a chord. It sticks in my head and often something related to it comes to pass."

"What sort of things . . . er . . . do you mind if I write this down?"

"You're not going to put this in your book, are you?" James looked alarmed, then broke into a grin. "Just teasing . . . I'd be honoured if you quoted me."

"OK, tell me more. What does this mean to you? I don't mean the signs themselves; I mean the fact that this is happening and repeatedly so?"

"A couple of weeks ago, I kept hearing the word 'delicatessen' everywhere. It'd be on TV, or it would jump out at me from an advert in a magazine or newspaper. I'd see it somewhere where I couldn't remember seeing it before. And it was definitely 'delicatessen' – not deli. So, I looked it up in the dictionary. Of course I know what a deli is, but I wanted to know if there was something more for me, if it was trying to tell me something. Webster's said: 'ready-to-eat food products, cooked meats and prepared salads.'"

"Well? Did that mean something to you?" I laughed while finishing the last few bites of my apricot turnover.

"Yes, and no. Then I thought more about it – or rather I didn't think – I just let words and random thoughts come to me: Eclectic, discerning, dilettante, connoisseur. I still don't know *why* I kept seeing the word, but I paid attention to it and wondered how it applied to my life or perhaps to some situation. I still don't know, but I trust it.

"I firmly believe that present and future are tied together and that symbols can foreshadow an event or circumstance..."

"But its not a 'psychic' phenomena, right?" I added, finishing his sentence.

"Right, its just information. I think these kinds of things are just a way the unconscious communicates to the conscious. I think our unconscious knows the whole picture and fits in the parts the conscious self is missing. It can be through a dream, a symbol, word, or a sign. It's just like in a dream – a waking dream – it has the same resonance.

"One morning, I woke up with the word 'pusillanimous' in my head; it was literally pounding. I'd heard it before – probably one of those words you hear on spelling bees – but had no idea what it meant. Well, it turned out the root of the word stems from *punus* (very small) and *animus* (spirit), with an interpretation of 'lacking courage and resolution; timidity, and 'weak in spirit.'

"That time, I knew instantly why I was hearing the word; I was in the middle of a situation that required me to truly stand up for myself, though not in an egotistical way. I needed to be strong in spirit and master spiritual force. As soon as I had that insight, I stopped hearing the word."

"And did you follow through?" I asked. "It's one thing to make the connection, to have the 'ah-ha', or hear the word, but if you don't follow through, what's the point?"

James looked thoughtful.

"Yes, I believe I did. Perhaps not as strongly as I would have liked, but much more so than if I hadn't heard the word at all. Plus, now I know for sure that these kinds of insights, images and words carry useful messages or point the way, so I pay more attention and also find they happen more when I do."

I told James how I had noticed the same thing: " The more I use them the more they happen. It's as if my unconscious – if that's what it is – just wants the acknowledgement and then the channel opens wider; especially so if the 'gift' of intuition is wisely used."

We hugged and said our goodbyes. James said he would call later if he thought of some more examples, or if he woke up the next day with "dendrogram" in his head. I told him not to call *too* early in the morning!

I remained on my bale for a while longer and wrote a few more notes, thinking especially about the open channel and James' exponential synchronicities. I concluded it works in a similar way to gratitude. Gratitude opens the heart, so perhaps acknowledgement opens the unconscious. It is the same spiritual law as giving. Giving opens up the way to receiving, like the law of tithing, which opens up a channel of abundance.

I also questioned, as I had before, whether such signs were really good or from the so-called psychic plane. How would I know? How would anyone know?

Then I suddenly realised that I do "just know"; I trust it, it feels good and settles in my body without question. Something my friend Maggie had said to me came to mind:

"There is an inner voice that is clear and clean. That inner voice is the voice that speaks up for my growth and my integrity. The body signal is that it gives energy rather than taking energy away."

I knew that was true, so no more inner questioning. "Never argue with a hunch," I remembered the affirmation on my fridge door, written in 1925 by one Florence Scovel Shinn. With that, I climbed down off the hay bale, dusted off my skirt and headed into the crowded market aisles to forage amidst the bountiful veggies, with a hunch (or was it a desire?) that I would find the freshest, firmest tomatoes.

It was late in the season here in Northern New Mexico for tomatoes, but after a very dry spring and early summer they were just ripening. I bought several pounds of mixed yellows and reds, biting into one and spraying tomato juice and seeds everywhere. I berated myself for wearing a white blouse on a day during which I knew I'd get offered tasty samples and be eating as I strolled along.

I paused to squirt water from my water bottle onto the stain before it dried. That, of course, left me soaking wet and in more of a mess, so I headed back towards the parking lot and my car, remembering the pile of clothes in a bag I was planning to take to the charity shop. A quick change and I could go back to finish my shopping. Just as I reached my car, a vintage Volvo was pulling out of the space next to mine, but it suddenly stopped.

"Hi, Carly! What you doing?"

"Greg! Perfect!" I grinned, looking down at the mess I was in. "Would be you, I just spilled something on my shirt and was about to get a clean one."

"Really, Carly, you look just fine."

"Well, I feel silly," I responded. "Hey, I still haven't interviewed you for my book."

"About wet shirts?"

"No, the Guidance book!"

"I don't get guidance," he grinned.

"Yes, you do, I know quite well you do, in fact you've told me numerous stories about how you run your business with the help of spiritual guidance and intuition."

"Well, that's true," he conceded, pretending to be self-effacing.

"So, how about a story for the book?"

"Which one?"

Greg and I have been best friends for eighteen years and tease one another like brother and sister.

"How about the dream story?" I suggested, instantly recalling a story he'd told me ten years earlier.

Forgetting for a moment about my shirt, we slouched against his car in the parking lot and I began to take notes as Greg started his story:

"I was looking for a new manager and had a dream about someone I'd seen previously in a restaurant, someone who hadn't even applied for the job. I woke from the dream and decided to ask him if he was interested. He said 'yes' and so I hired him the following week; he went on to save a major account, which at that time was responsible for most of our income.

"Another time, some people on staff advised me to hire a particular person and I got a strong 'no' feeling, but felt pressured and hired him anyway. Three months later we had to fire him. I always know and trust my intuition. It works."

"Have you always been this clear?" I asked.

"Sometimes I'm not, but it really started about fifteen years ago when I was travelling in Europe, I was in Austria and had to make a decision about a place to stay. I literally heard, 'Yah' and 'Nein' in my head!"

"You mean you actually heard 'yes' and 'no' in German?"

"Precisely, for the whole week!"

"I remember you went to Greece on that same trip. Did you get guidance in Greek?"

"Its all Greek to me!"

I should have known better than to ask.

"Seriously, though," Greg continued, "I do trust my intuition. I recognise when I'm 'on.' Everything seems clearer and brighter. It's as if I can see better; everything is lighter, and I even feel lighter, like the air around seems less heavy. And sometimes, I don't even have to do anything, guidance just happens to me."

"Explain," I prompted, this time not knowing what he was about to say.

"Well, like one time I was researching a film I wanted to make and hoped to meet with a particular person. Everyone told me I wouldn't be able to find him as he'd been out of touch for three months, seemed no-one knew where he was. My entire focus had been on finding this man, so as it finally appeared that I couldn't, and since I'd been working non-stop for a while, I decided to take a break and head for the beach. I was living in Oregon at the time and had been driving for about twenty minutes, when I realised I was actually driving in the wrong direction. I was heading towards Mt. Hood, another favourite place of mine, but I knew it was snowed-in up there! So I turned around and went back the other way

"About another thirty minutes later I woke up, as if from a dream, and realised I was once more headed for the mountains; I had no memory of exiting the freeway and turning around to go back the other way. I turned around again. About an hour later I 'awoke' to find that somehow I was once again driving into the mountains and was almost at Mt. Hood. I gave up

– it was too late for the beach anyway – so I drove into the only place you could go, which was the Lodge. I walked around a bit, and then went back to the car to sit and think awhile. A short time later I went back into the Lodge and immediately ran into the man I had been looking for all along! It turned out he had just gotten married; he was in a really ecstatic state and had just dropped by for a few minutes to show the place to his new wife. I was completely re-energised!

"Another time, I wanted to say goodbye to an old girlfriend in New York City, so I went to her apartment (she didn't have a phone), but found she wasn't home. I was headed back to the West Coast the next morning and really wanted to see her before leaving, so decided to walk around for a while and then try her apartment again, but she still wasn't back. I finally gave up and headed onto the subway to make my way to where I was staying. At Times Square I had to change trains and was walking in one of the many connecting subway tunnels, when we literally collided into each other! I had been looking right and she left."

"There's definitely something bigger than our eyes can see or ears can hear," I suggested.

"Precisely!" Greg agreed, as we concluded our conversation.

He drove off – I believe in the right direction.

Chapter 9

BIG GUIDANCE

"There's always something"
[Gilda Radner]

Sitting in the shade beneath the heavily laden branches of Marty's peach tree was the optimal way to pick and eat the luscious fruit, catch up on one another's news, and find some relief from the high-desert heat. Marty and I thought we first met on the island of Erraid off the western Scottish coast in 1979, but there's a photograph in *Faces of Findhorn* clearly showing both of us meeting and greeting people off the Cluny Hill bus at some point earlier. It would appear that on that day we passed one another without knowing, but now twenty-something years later we both live in New Mexico; Marty with a peach tree in her back yard, and me with an apricot tree in mine.

Marty had invited me over to pick peaches and tell me about her new job. She had been a kindergarten teacher since her Findhorn days and had just landed a new teaching post, this time with first and second grade students in a Charter school.

"Why did you leave your job after all this time?" I asked her.

"I knew in a non-verbal way that I wanted to change jobs and had been looking for some time, but hadn't realised I was really ready to quit. Then in the last week of school in May I had this overwhelming urge to pack up my entire classroom – everything. I usually tidy it up of course, and take home my personal things, but this was different. My mind lagged behind, but my instinct to pack up everything was overpowering.

"Later on in the week I knew I was ready to leave. I had been miserable in that school for some time, and realised it couldn't be the Divine Idea for my life to be working hours and hours every week with such a heavy heart. I reached a point where I said clearly to God, 'OK, my life is in your hands, show me what you want me to do. You take over.' I think it was the first time in my life when I really, really surrendered. I even added a postscript to God saying, 'even if you want me to go back to the old job.'"

"And then did you just sit back and trust?" I asked.

"Well, yes, pretty much. I found an affirmation by Florence Scovel Shinn, which really helped and I said it many times a day: *'The long arm of God reaches over people and conditions, controlling this situation and protecting my interests.'* She wrote that in 1928 and gave affirmations and prayer 'treatments' for people. She was quite a remarkable lady."

"I know you were offered the new job this week, but what happened in between?"

"Because I put myself out there in God's hands, I learned to totally trust. This time I said 'no' to directing my own path, fully knowing that God *would* take care of it. As I am only a few years away from retirement in the public schools, I even knew that God would take care of my retirement needs. It was a total exercise in trust, and I'd never before done it quite this way. If we are really here on earth to fulfil our soul's purpose and we just say 'God, take over' then we must assume that what works out is what is meant to be. And, of course, you *do* do everything you can, but to a point. Leave some space for God to work. I don't think its God's job to create pot holes or to trip us up."

"Right," I commented, "it seems you reached a point of no fear, and that the absolute trust and fearlessness combined to allow the outworking of the perfect plan for you."

"Absolutely! I think fear somehow sabotages our trust in Divine guidance. I know. I've experienced that for sure."

"Me, too. It's as if letting in the doubts exacerbate the fears and the two combined nullify the guidance. So, how *did* you work with your doubts and fears? They must have come up."

"Yes, they did, but again I felt this extraordinary trusting strength. And I kept coming across sayings and wisdom that helped me every time I faltered. Like in one of St. Paul's letters to the Philippians in the New Testament: *'Do not worry about anything, but in all things make your requests known to God in prayer and petition with thanksgiving.'*"

"Ah, I see the hand of gratitude again. I've spoken to a lot people while writing this book, and many have spoken about gratitude playing a part in defining and following guidance – whatever the form of guidance. Gratitude opens the heart and it seems that opening the heart allows all the senses to freely open."

"Yes," Marty confirmed, "it's part of the laws of manifestation we learned at Findhorn: 'God knows your needs, even before you do, trust in him and give thanks.'"

"So how did the job actually manifest?"

"Well, a couple of weeks later, I saw it advertised and applied, so nothing particularly unusual. I was interviewed twice, and on my second interview did feel I should mention I was hoping to go to Scotland – to Findhorn – for the 40th Birthday Reunion. I realised that could jeopardise my chance of winning the position, but felt intuitively that I must ask if they could possibly honour my plans in mid-term. It turned out that the Principal herself had been invited to a very special family reunion at the start of the school year and had had to turn it down. I thought for a moment she might turn me down just because of personal jealously, but no, she understood completely how important it was for me, even though she could not go to her own reunion. I was offered the job and really feel very good about working with someone who is so 'big' in her wisdom and thinking."

We took a break to eat more peaches and drink iced tea. Marty was soon in a flow of conversation about calling upon spiritual guidance for major life transitions:

"I had been living at Findhorn for several years and was leading a dream workshop. One day, I was inspired to tell about a dream of my own which puzzled me, it was something I rarely did as I usually used the students' dreams as examples, not my own. In the dream, I had received an anonymous gift – a package of some kind – so I opened it and found it was a leather-bound book of maps. One of my students turned the tables on me and suggested I take a moment in the class to become the dream, perhaps to 'become' the book of maps and to speak from that perspective.

"As I spoke, I felt that something in me wanted to move on, though I don't remember exactly what I said at the time, just the feeling, and also a feeling of not knowing. However, I'd worked with dreams enough to know that it was OK not to know, and left it at that. It was four or five months later I realised that was the very first inkling I had of stirrings to leave the community, and it illustrated a new impulse even before I felt it consciously. Again, that was a non-verbal form of guidance, and again, my unconscious was well ahead of my conscious."

I drove from Marty's house thinking a lot about "big" guidance – the sort required for life transforming issues like moving home, beginning or ending a relationship, or changing career. My investigation into guidance sometimes wavered when it came to "big" guidance, yet those are the very times that guidance is needed most. Marty's story of surrender and letting God guide, even in an unknown way, opened up the possibilities even further. What if there is *no* guidance?

"There's always something," a voice in my head intruded my thoughts and I laughed out loud when I realised this was precisely one of the "voices" I hear that seems to come from elsewhere, from someplace beyond the usual clamour and static of internal dialogue. I personally have had many experiences of big guidance, and though in the heat of the moment – amidst fears of change or doubts about material security – I sometimes forget that the guidance is always available, it always is.

My friend Karin chats with God regularly and any doubts she has are usually erased by the voice of the Goddess reminding Karin of that invincible support. "Have I *ever* let you down?" she will ask in a slightly quizzical tone.

But what if God doesn't show up? I thought about this, remembering several occasions when things didn't turn out as hoped, despite my prayers and petitions.

"Doubt!" came the answer, "Remember, God doesn't create potholes, but you might. Eliminate doubt." I had an image of the alien Borg from *Star Trek*. "Resistance is futile!" the invincible half-man, half-machine character would claim. I decided to pit doubt and fear against the Borg – if I couldn't eliminate them, the Borg certainly would – and adopted a Borgonian sub-personality for this very purpose.

I arrived home to a voice mail from my good friend and massage therapist, Jordan, reminding me I had an appointment the following afternoon.

When I arrived, he told me he and his partner were considering going into partnership with another couple to buy a cafe. I asked him how he had come to the decision that a cafe would be a good idea?

"I'd been putting out there the desire for something new in my life; another form of livelihood that would fit with what I am already doing, that would add to it without taking anything away."

I knew the cafe he spoke of; a popular and eclectic gathering space and art gallery favoured by writers and artists. It serves delicious teas and elixirs as well as mouth-watering berry pies infused with Chinese herbs.

"So, how did you come to the decision?" I asked again. Jordan's answer surprised me; again opening up a new way of looking at the many different forms guidance can take.

"I have been declaring who I am as a 'possibility of being'. In other words, instead of deciding what I'm going to *do*, I have chosen to *be* . . ."

I had to interrupt him for a moment, intrigued by what he meant by "declaring" himself and "possibility of being." I asked for some clarity.

"It's a term borrowed from Landmark Education, which grew out of Werner Erhardt's est programme of the 1970's. So, I have been declaring who I am as 'courageous, self-expressed and *being* my word.' Being who I am generating myself to be at the core. Additionally, I have created possibilities for domains in my life that I want to manage. For example, using this terminology, my career domain is called 'expression explosion', it includes the possibility of being playful, alive, and in community. Out of this arose the opportunity to purchase the cafe. It clearly fits into my 'possibilities of being.' And you know the rest of the story."

I did indeed! And I wished Jordan many blessings on his new venture, while also wondering whether he'd still have time to do massage in the future. With that thought, I lay face down on his massage table and began to let go of the stresses of the day under Jordan's skilful hands.

That evening, I received an e-mail from Amantha in Ireland. She had been through many changes in her life over the last few years and I had asked her how she found the courage, inspiration and discipline to follow her guidance, especially "big" guidance? Her response was simple:

> For some reason I seem to go with it. It's as if that is the only 'real' energy and all the rest is 'dream time.' There has never been a question of not following it once I have recognised it and allowed it to penetrate within.

Her words sent a zing through my body, even though I was sleepy. *Real* energy, I knew exactly what she meant; that sharp, crisp awareness, something my friend Bruce calls 'a snap of awareness.' Something I experience as solid, fully formed, decisive, and impeccable. I closed my eyes awhile before opening them again to reread Amantha's words:

> There has never been a question of not following it once I have recognised it and allowed it to penetrate within.

Sleep, I knew, would allow my own clear moments to penetrate.

∞∞∞

The following morning I met with Elaine over coffee in the tropical garden store, surrounded by colourful and luscious plants in vibrant oranges, corals, pinks, reds, ochre and salmon; a perfect setting for chatting with a fellow author. Elaine has written numerous books, is an avid bicycle rider and loves adventure of every kind, however, on this morning she was dealing with a dental problem!

"Hello, Carly, sorry I'm late," she said as she breezed into the cafe. "There's always something! My tooth – the one I just had crowned – well, the crown fell out."

No need to put the rest of the painful story in this book, except to say that Elaine instantly saw it as a segue into our planned conversation about guidance.

"You cannot find guidance without, it is within, otherwise its first the dentist, then the refrigerator hum – whatever it is, if you're waiting for the world to give it to you, it won't. Life is like a mirror reflecting the image of one's inner beliefs. I write morning pages each day, usually in the morning, but sometimes in the evening. They are my touchstone for the day. I ask for guidance and get answers. The guidance is the clear voice, not the static on the overcrowded channel. Sometimes I whine a bit in my pages, so I stop for a moment to read a poem by Rumi or Rilke and that shuts up the whiney voice. I set up my own stumbling blocks and the morning pages allow me to find out where I am and show how I can answer the fears. Ultimately, I come into the gratitude, and say, 'thank you God.'

"I receive guidance through visual images and also through nature in a Wordsworth-like sense. I have a corner of my garden as a saturnine garden; a place to be melancholy, to cry, to be alone with myself."

Elaine and I spoke for a while about her latest book, *From Calcutta with Love*, an exquisite compilation of love letters between her father and mother during WWII, based upon which she is also busy producing a one-act play.

"Guidance also comes to me through dreams," she continued. "Two dreams especially come to mind right now: both about my mother who died last year. In the first, some years ago, she was showing me a large road map with two routes. The northern route was longer and harder but more effective, the southern route looked easier but I knew in the dream it was not the one to take. Mother was pointing to the north route and I heard the words, 'It is not easy, but it is the road.' That is the one I have taken.

"In the second dream, shortly before she died, my mother was standing at the top of a flight of stairs dressed in a very beautiful gold and brown fleur-de-lys silk gown. I didn't really hear the words, but she conveyed in some way that 'Elaine would be alright.' And, that, too, has been so.

"I believe my mother stayed alive so she could see the completed book. The publishers sent her a copy even before me – she died one week later."

Elaine's eyes filled with tears for a moment and we sat together in that unique silence between sadness and sweetness, before finishing our coffee and saying our goodbye's. As I watched her drive away from the cafe, I felt sure she would spend some time that day in her saturnine garden.

A few days later, I had the opportunity to be with a friend for whom guidance and faith proved primary during probably the most difficult experience anyone could have: The death of a child. Jean's stepdaughter, Naomi, had died of cancer three years earlier, at just nineteen years of age. I had just finished reading Jean's husband's poignant book, *A Heart Traced in Sand*, about their family's journey with their beloved daughter's illness and her dying; a book full of true stories of faith, challenges, grace, intuitions, knowings – and not knowings.

Jean and I spoke about the way guidance unfolds in her life:

"I think that openness to the possibility of receiving information from guidance or intuition is vitally important. In order to listen with our full attention to what might come to us, we must have complete faith in its validity, and courage to remain open to its gifts.

"Sometimes guidance comes to me in dreams; I will often awake with the sense that something powerful has been revealed to me. A general feeling of warmth and well being comes into my body. It's not always immediately clear what significance the dream contains, so I make an effort to remember and sort out the events and details. If I awake in the middle of the night following such a dream, I force myself to write it down; otherwise the memory of it will usually be quite hazy the next day.

"I have received numerous messages and assurances through dreams from friends and loved ones who have passed on into the spiritual world. They have let me know that they are in a beautiful place and happy to be free of their physical body. They have given me inspirational messages for my own life, too.

"Sometimes, a dream may reveal something about my life that I hadn't been completely conscious of before, or point out some aspect that I may need to work on. For example, I may dream about being in some very restricted place or situation, such as an enclosed room with no doors and no way out, and I interpret this as a time to look at what limitations I experience and how I am unconsciously allowing them to limit me in my life.

"I have had dreams about individuals with whom I have been out of touch for a long time and within a short time of the dream they reappear in my life!"

I asked Jean if her experience of guidance and intuition were similar.

"I think that guidance and intuition often work together, like when I receive guidance about something and my intuition steps in to help clarify or illuminate whatever the guidance is showing me. To me, guidance comes from a source outside myself such as from the spiritual world. Intuition seems to be something that arises from within myself.

"They work together in ways that allow me to receive useful information. I often feel that the combination of these two direct me to be 'in the right place at the right time,' whether it be finding something material – like a parking place in town – or meeting someone important to my life in a situation that could be called a 'coincidence.'"

I noted something she said about numbers:

"The birth date of our daughter who passed on into the spiritual world was 1-11-80. Our younger daughter's birth date is 11-11-86. After our older daughter's passing, whenever we travelled and stayed in a hotel, our room number was usually either 111 or 1111. We always took this as confirmation from another realm."

∞∞∞

My friend, Denise, who works as a landscape gardener, touched upon the heart of how guidance weaves through our lives, even when we don't consciously know it:

I am daily watching myself step more fully into life – moving from the back seat of the 'bus' into the driver's seat of my life. I attribute this wholly to a growing sense of trust in myself – my inner knowing – and the courage to let that knowing determine the course of my life.

I am discovering a more 'real' and authentic me and the creative, intuitive flow in my life. I see creativity and intuition as intricately interwoven, if not the same thing. I feel myself stretching and pushing like a chick breaking through a shell. I go through bursts of allowing the flow and I come alive each time. I find joy and the thrill of creation in writing, growing plants, creating beautiful spaces inside and out, art, and speaking from the heart – whether with friends, or with strangers in line at the grocery store.

I feel such certainty of the importance of this 'flow' and it's impact. If I choose what is in my heart in any moment, whether I call it intuition or inner knowing, I can turn the moment around and bring it to life.

When I remember to be present, to come 'home' to centre, to listen within, the fears of what the world thinks of me become thin, like paper dolls. They become powerless and almost endearing in their paper impersonations. One of my most interesting insights is a dawning of awareness of how asleep I've been, back there in the back of the bus! How weird it is to realise how I had thought I was participating, and how funny to see and feel what it really takes to give myself to this life. It is also sobering to see that I still don't fully get it. For the first time in my life, I feel change within and increasing awareness.; the type of shift and growth I've yearned for my entire life, through all the spiritual teachings and searching. The source of this change is undoubtedly due to my increasing willingness to navigate from the heart, to let my intuitive self do the driving.

Intuition is often so subtle and I always wanted fireworks! However, hindsight shows me that intuition was always there, quietly and with calm certainty, humble, yet true and powerful in its truth. Sometimes it is so unobtrusive I can easily choose to label it insignificant, if I even notice it at all.

Yet, when I'm willing to cooperate with and use intuition – can I ever find parking! The little things, like parking, are easiest. The lower the perceived risk, the more miracles I witness. Clearly, I must detach from desired outcomes to allow intuitive guidance into the driver's seat. I've seen so many graceful and amazing solutions, things I never could have orchestrated so beautifully. They happen only when I get out of the way, quieten my judgments and allow inner knowing to go to work on the situation.

One of the biggest and funniest insights for me is the realisation that I was pretending to be small and insignificant; I am now beginning to get more comfortable with courage. Regardless of external circumstances, the internal experience of choosing courage is beyond comparison.

Denise's courage is inspiring and real and I have witnessed some of the changes her new-found courage has brought into her life. Similarly, my friend Stephen observes how guidance is always available and especially within nature and in places of great beauty and power.

For me, guidance is awareness, which may be simply seeing life symbolically, and awareness that nothing happens without reason. There are all kinds of manifestations available that guide me. From the perspective that all is Spirit or God, it's as if once I drop the ego belief, that 'I'm in control,' I reconnect to the existence of God guiding me toward transformation.

Guidance comes out of paying attention to what is being mirrored. It comes in the myriad guises of other humans and from the presence of our animal brothers and birds. It can come through the elements – through the wind and the rain – and through the moon, the stars and the planets. It can come in both the waking dream and the asleep dream. It is everywhere, in every facet of existence when I place my awareness on what appears to be 'real' and discern it from the duality of illusion.

Really, I have no name for this, though perhaps the hugest piece of 'guidance' I've ever received was a powerful voice which manifested itself when I was at the Pyramid of Quetzalcoatl in Teotihuacan, Mexico. I had been struggling with the act of forgiveness in regard to my parents and inwardly asked a simple question, in this case, 'Why didn't my father take me fishing?' From this simple question a door broke open and a wave of emotions flowed out. Once I'd felt this emotional outburst, a voice became perceptible which, in very simple terms, explained the entire energetic dynamics of my parent's relationship and why they made the choices they made.

Once I actually understood this energy there was no longer any reason not to forgive them both. From that moment forward my life dramatically changed for the better. One could say this inspirational act of forgiveness which was gifted to me by guides beyond my comprehension has altered my destiny and I continue to reap the rewards of guidance.

Chapter 10

RECAPITULATION

"Friends, I do believe that we are born to swim our own path.
I've been in mine deep and away while my neighbours walked
the road of stone. This took my breath away.
The will of the heart knows its course. Love is the power!"
[Jennifer Esperanza]

Three days before I e-mailed the manuscript of this book to Findhorn Press I sat at my computer feeling that I'd missed something. Wondering if there was something else that needed to be included, and if there was, what was it? Even though I'm a writer and broadcaster, I'm not always one for lots of words. I had felt like I'd said enough, like there was no need for more. Silence for me is truly *golden*. Yet I sensed there was one more thing; not another chapter, maybe just a page, or a few paragraphs. I noticed myself wondering, even beginning to fret a little as I couldn't put my finger on what it might be; nothing was coming to me through meditation or intuition. I thought I should maybe go back and read the book from the beginning again, or maybe a brisk walk would do it. I laughed at myself.

Then the phone rang. It was my friend Genoa, calling to tell me he'd just sent an e-mail he hoped I would read before sending off the book to the publisher. I told him how I had just been sitting pondering, and not getting anywhere! We laughed at the irony of it, and talked for a few minutes.

"Maybe there's something in the e-mail," he suggested.

I put the phone down and read Genoa's mail; a further, remarkable insight he had about his work with the Human Design System, which I added to the chapter where I had written about the conversation we'd had in person a few days earlier. But still, this was not quite the conclusion for the book. Maybe the next phone call, I thought, and decided to make a cup of tea to clear my head. Sitting on my patio outside in the late afternoon sun, I was hoping a flock of geese would fly by and inspire me. A sign from nature, I thought, that's what I need right now! My neighbour's black cat chose this moment to idly pad across the top of the garden wall by the apple tree. Cats . . . witches . . . Halloween . . . free associative thinking just didn't cut the mustard this time!

Refreshed, I returned inside, sat back down at my computer and continued to stare at it, occasionally writing down any and all thoughts that came into my head, just to prime the creative pump.

The phone rang again, this time it was my ten-year-old son, Joss, who's always an inspiration; telling me he'd lost another tooth and reminding me that tooth fairy charges had gone 'way' up since the last baby tooth fell out. I suggested that as he was at dad's house he should consult the resident tooth fairy there.

∞∞∞

"With no fear and no defences, in the absolute safety of absolute vulnerability, there is only the moment in God – and it's as simple as that."

[Elizabeth Papapetrou]

Hearing the phone ring twenty minutes later, I almost didn't answer it, because I was, finally, beginning to get into a flow. However, in a split-second the voice of intuition said "get it," so I did. This time it was my Findhorn friend Elizabeth who lives in Florida.

She had called to ask my advice about something and we talked and laughed for a good ten minutes. I told her I had to finish the book – *tonight* – and had been sitting here with writer's block most of the afternoon.

"I know I'm missing something," I told her, "I can feel it." Wondering if she may be able to help, I read her the chapter headings and subtitles to give her an overview.

"Did you say anything about how guidance comes in the moment?" She asked.

"Well, yes, in many and various ways," I replied, slightly hesitant, sensing she was onto something.

"Do you have something to add?" I asked, suddenly very interested.

"Well, what I feel is that all these other forms of guidance are wonderful ways of talking with God sort of 'on the telephone.' However, the infinite divine that is God is at the core of all beings, and full acceptance of that truth prepares us to embody the divine expression in the human world which we call the Christed state. That experience – that truth – is found only in the moment, in the infinite Now."

"Can you explain in simpler words?"

"Hmmm, that's difficult. Wait a minute! I know. Let's think of our presence in the manifest world like a car driving along the highway of life and our Personality – our human identity – is in the back seat. In the driver's seat is our Higher Self, the fully empowered, divinely interconnected, greater Us that exists beyond the narrowly focused humanness of personality. If Personality is at peace with Higher Self driving, then our life flows effortlessly with the purposeful, multi-dimensional, unfolding of creation. We've all experienced at least a little of this: Those moments, hours, or even days and weeks, when we are our purpose and the universe is absolutely in service to us as we are in service to all, and the fluid inter-connection of all life is obvious and imminent. The idea of external guidance at such times seems almost ridiculous!

"Of course, most of the time the Ego aspect of Personality does not believe that Higher Self is navigating all worlds and all situations perfectly for us. All it can see is that it appears to be in a runaway car with no driver. Not being able to move into the driver's seat itself (after all, Higher Self is there)

Ego instead lunges over the back of the seat, grabs the wheel and tries to steer for itself, believing it is in great danger. Unfortunately, Ego knows nothing about driving this particular car, cares little for the interconnection of all life, and disdains the perfect unfolding of creation. All it sees is imminent danger. Thus, we often find ourselves lurching from one potential disaster to another with Ego wildly spinning the steering wheel this way and that, justifying to itself its need to continue 'driving' by pointing out experiences in the past that 'prove' the dangers, which it then projects into the future as situations to be avoided at all cost.

"Balance is lost, the moment is forgotten, regrets from the past and fears of the future reign while Ego tries to apply the brakes and order life through rational thinking. This ends up as a carefully controlled, white-knuckle ride with full conscious attention paid to the past and the future to keep the car on the road – not to mention a lot of angry honking on the horn to alert other drivers on the road!"

I fell about laughing as I listened to Elizabeth speak, seeing myself far too clearly driving down the highway of life just as she described.

"Have you ever let Higher Self take over the driving?" I asked.

"Yes, there was a time of grace when I went from a dyed-in-the-wool atheist to direct experience of the divine in a heartbeat. It was like the solid ground I had been standing on my entire life fell away and I struggled just to find something real to base my life on. I did not find that reality in conventional spiritual wisdom or books, in divination or any other guidance; I found it in what seemed like accidental surrender of fear and absolute acceptance of the moment. It lasted several weeks.

"Later, my ego gradually crept back into my life and I started living a parody of a state of Grace as my ego had 'learned' what that state might involve being and doing. Thus, I became subject again to the ministrations of fear and kind of fell off the mountain – or more accurately, fell out of the moment.

"These days, as I let go my definitions of self and the world, I find myself 'there' more and more. I believe that every one of us spends portions of each day in this Christed state where our human and Divine selves are one, but perhaps we don't notice because it is just seems like absorption in the moment. We are so trained to envision and thus expect enlightened moments to match our projections and concepts of God, replete with angels, guides, saints and avatars! Yet, really, no concept can express the truth of God, it can only be experienced and such experience is special to each person, and each moment.

"So, to recap, I believe it is our destiny to be Christed, for all of us human beings to be fully Divine and fully human at the same time. Key to the Christing is letting go of the past and allowing the future to unfold, as it will. With no fear and no defences, in the absolute safety of absolute vulnerability, there is only the moment in God – and it's as simple as that."

We were both silent as we let this sink in.

"Elizabeth," I began, noticing how her words reminded me of the children, of their simultaneous innocence and awareness, "there is a lot of talk of special children being born now that demonstrate this truth. Have you heard about these children and what they bring to us?"

"Yes, it's truly wonderful, isn't it? What appears to distinguish these children is that they retain pre-birth knowledge of Divine truth and resist the societal pressures to conform to established, comfortable and predictable ways of being that ultimately 'normalise' us and take us away from the truth of our Highest Self. They embody innocence, vulnerability and trust in the play of creation, plus infinite Divine wisdom in a way that is breathtaking to those of us who have struggled in the world to make sense of this shattered truth. However, we can all choose to become these special children, playing in trust with the world at any moment we choose, if we but let go and choose to re-capitulate, to surrender again and, rather than 'let God', 'stand revealed as God.'

"Whenever I feel the weight of human life pulling me down, I like to go down to the Itchetucknee River, a beautiful six-mile stretch of slow flowing water, which leaps into being from nine springs here in North Florida. There I can rent a giant inner tube and float down the river, just letting the gentle whirls and eddies carry me as they will. It is a fabulous, living analogy for life: Floating serenely on the current of unfolding creation with no need for paddles. Just constantly changing scenery of breathtaking beauty, and great wildlife!

"The Itchetucknee experience even offers a counterpart to reincarnation; the State Park busses you back to the headwaters at the end of the trip – for free – and you can start all over again!"

We both laughed, and I told Elizabeth that I would definitely accept her invitation to visit – especially if we could go inner tubing!

"That's a great metaphor," I concluded, "just shows that if we can trust the flow of our lives instead of always fighting against the current, our lives become effortless, simpler and more childlike."

∞∞∞

"There was a certain point where I came to acknowledge the force, the wisdom and the playfulness of intuition in my life. Now, I roll with the paradoxes of life. I love the word 'crone' and I like the idea of cackling with the paradoxes and the ever-replenishing mystery and miracles of life."

[Shama Beach]

The following morning I woke up early and headed out to the farmers' market. Even though I had a book deadline 24 hours later, I knew without question that the market was where I needed to be.

I had been there hardly five minutes when I ran into a long-time friend, Patty, who lives in the mid-west and stays in New Mexico in the summer. It turned out she was leaving the following day to go home. Our meeting didn't surprise me; we've been doing this dance for many years. I knew that in her hometown she spent time with women from her circle of faith, helping them to come closer to their own inner wisdom. She rarely used the word "intuition" as in her community it had connotations of being something a little too metaphysical. Patty had long been a bridge between more conservative thinkers and the very individualistic characters in her adopted state.

"How do you speak about these things to someone who may be a little cautious?" I asked her.

"I'm always careful how I describe this. But also, I feel that intuition is not the end of it all. I believe it is *one* of the ways we are guided towards God and from *there* we make wise choices, decisions and evaluations. Wisdom is an attribute of God, and intuition is a gift."

Patty and I hugged warmly, headed off in opposite directions, having agreed to meet for lunch the following June when she returned to Santa Fe.

I stopped by many booths, picking up tomatoes, Jonathan apples, green, red and orange sweet peppers, a large bag of organic salad greens, another jar of lavender face cream, and a cup of de-caf coffee, sampling as I went. As I reached the hay bales, there was my good friend, Shama. We had been hoping to connect since the early summer to speak about intuition and guidance, but had never quite managed to find a mutual time; besides, we both knew we would meet if it were meant to be. Shama is a respected elder in our community, a marvellous storyteller and self-described "crone."

"There you are!" She exclaimed as she saw me approaching with my coffee. "I thought we'd find each other one day. I still have that questionnaire you sent me! Are you still writing the book? I hope I'm not too late." She moved over to make room for me on a straw bale.

"Shama, this is the perfect day, I'm e-mailing the manuscript tomorrow. I would love to include you if you want to be included."

"Well, yes," she said, handing me a poster about a group poetry evening she had organised, entitled *Dancing Between Worlds*.

"Have you danced between the worlds all your life Shama?"

"Almost," she chuckled, "I think the first time was when I was visiting Japan as a young woman and was in early pregnancy. I got some terrible stomach bug, but the doctor there insisted I had appendicitis and if I didn't go to the hospital immediately my appendix would burst. I didn't believe him. I don't know how I knew, but I absolutely knew I didn't have appendicitis and I certainly didn't want to end up in a strange hospital in a foreign country, where I did not know the language and would have my appendix removed for no reason! That's when I first learned how to trust my body, my inner knowing, and myself.

"There was a certain point where I came to acknowledge the force, the wisdom and the *playfulness* of intuition in my life. I stopped taking it all so seriously. One day, a friend gave me a piece of pottery she'd brought back from Taos, New Mexico. I lived in New York City – New Mexico was another world away. Some time later, I was walking between 83rd Street and Amsterdam, when I clearly heard my inner voice say, 'Taos, yes, that's where I'm going!' And I moved there the following December.

"Now, I roll with the paradoxes of life. I love the word 'crone' and I like the idea of cackling with the paradoxes and the ever-replenishing mystery and miracles of life. I recognise the joy, the urgency, and the pain of the present times. I feel it all, and am involved with it all. I do what I can and let the moment guide me."

Shama's eyes shone as she turned to look at me. I stopped writing and our eyes met in that knowing place where no more words were necessary.

Just at that moment, the eleven o'clock train pulled noisily out of the little station, taking Saturday tourists to the nearby village of Lamy, on old tracks that were once used daily to deliver folks and freight to the old city.

We looked across to the train passing by just a hundred feet away; there were children jumping up and down on an open flatbed, waving excitedly. We waved back and watched as the caboose disappeared into the distant grove of golden trees, and I remembered the words of Thomas, the young boy from Bulgaria:

"Everything is happening exactly as it should. And remember, the time has arrived when innocence will prevail, when the Children will lead the way into the Light."

Gratitude filled my heart. I slipped my notebook back in my purse, and let my Higher Self drive me home.

BIBLIOGRAPHY

By authors related to the Findhorn Community

Bogliolo, Karin and Newfeld, Carly, *In Search of the Magic of Findhorn*, Findhorn Press 2002

Caddy, Eileen, *Flight into Freedom and Beyond*, Findhorn Press 2002

God Spoke to Me, Findhorn Press 1992

Opening Doors Within, Findhorn Press 1987

Be Still: Meditation for the Child Within, audio-tape, Findhorn Press 1981

Caddy, Peter, *In Perfect Timing*, Findhorn Press 1996

Findhorn Community, *The Findhorn Garden* (Findhorn Press: UK, Europe & Commonwealth; HarperCollins: rest of the world; 1975)

Maclean, Dorothy, *To Hear The Angels Sing* (Anthroposophic Press)

Choices of Love (Lindisfarne Books, 1998)

Communications with the Deva Kingdom, audio-tape, Findhorn Press 1981

Ogilvie Crombie, Robert (Roc), *Conversations with Pan*, audio-tape, Findhorn Press 1975

The Elemental Kingdom, audio-tape, Findhorn Press 1975

Spangler, David, *A Pilgrim in Aquarius* (Findhorn Press, 1996)

Everyday Miracles: The Inner Art of Manifestation (Bantam Books, 1996)

General bibliography or Reference

Boone, Steven, *A Heart Traced in Sand* (Santa Fe, NM Twin-Flames Publishing, 2002)

Castaneda, Carlos, *The Active Side of Infinity* (New York, HarperCollins, 1998)

Pinkerton, Elaine, *From Calcutta with Love* (Lubbock, TX, Texas Tech University Press 2002

Scott, Bruce, *Being Real: An Ongoing Decision* (Berkeley, CA North Atlantic Books, Frog Ltd., 2000)

Free the Children (to be published 2003)

Twyman, James, *Messages from Thomas: Raising Psychic Children*, Findhorn Press 2003

Web Sites and General Resources

The Findhorn Foundation:

www.findhorn.org

Genoa Bliven, Human Design System, Questa, NM, USA:

www.genoabliven.com

www.futurescape.org

Susan Feavearyear, Artemisia Herbs, Dixon, NM, USA:

artemisia@cybermesa.com

Joseph-Mark Cohen, Kabbalistic Astrologer :

www.treeoflifeschool.com

Amantha Murphy, Eire, Sacred Journeys:

www.ancientgoddesspilgrimage.com

www.sacredjourneys.com

New Mexico resources and information:

www.newmexico.org

Contact the author, Carly Newfeld:

carlynew@aol.com

ACKNOWLEDGMENTS

While walking in the hills near my home on December 24, 1961, I spontaneously experienced an illumination of all knowing, transcendent, loving, Divine Consciousness. I was thirteen years old. Returning to school after the Christmas break, we were asked to write an essay in English class about our holiday. I wrote two pages about my experience and excitedly gave it to the teacher; hoping I would receive an 'A' for such an inspiring and good piece of writing.

Two days later, my essay was returned marked "see me" in red ink, and the teacher sternly called me up in front of the class. She asked me from where I had copied such profane "drivel," accused me of lying when I insisted on the truth, and finally threw my essay in the rubbish bin. Faced with humiliation and disappointment, I momentarily withered. Then, as I walked back to my desk, a lightning bolt of clarity hit me and I realised that I would dedicate my life to proving that what I had experienced on the hill was real, and that I would guide others to find the loving divinity within, their authentic voice, and the courage to speak. This book is one small piece of the inner commitment I made that day in school.

There are many people to thank – some who contributed stories have asked to remain anonymous and so I will respect their wishes. Karin Bogliolo of Findhorn Press conceived the idea of a series called *The Findhorn Book of* . . . and I am honoured to be part of the first series; thank you dear Karin for your caring support, trust, and renewed friendship. Special gratitude to Findhorn Press editor, Elaine Harrison, who instantly caught the rhythm of the writing and was a perfect foil for my literary quirks; and to Thierry Bogliolo for his patience and presence.

Eileen Caddy, Dorothy Maclean, Peter Caddy, and David Spangler were the first people to show me that guidance manifested in different ways – though always from the same source: the route inside the heart. Their discipline and ability to model and teach what they experienced set my course. This book is a small token of gratitude for their work and lives in founding and developing the Findhorn Community. Special thanks to Findhorn Press for permission to quote from Peter's *In Perfect Timing*, and great gratitude to Dorothy for wonderful conversations on a sunlit mesa in Abiquiu, New Mexico and essential clarification of her early contact with the Devic world and the Findhorn story.

Thank you to everyone who shared intimate stories over tea, especially Marty Carroll, Jean Tobias Boone, Shama Beach, Denise Kanyon, Patty J., Yukiko Amaya, Jordan Minken, James Schultz, and Elaine Pinkerton. Thanks to friends around the country and the world whose voices of guidance and intuition are included here: Maggie Caffery, Amantha Murphy, Stephen Collector, Ed Bickford, and Robert Blakesley among them. I also had tea or 'cyber-tea' with many friends whose stories didn't make the final edit. Thank you for your willingness to participate and for being in my life. Thanks also to everyone who participated, though your story may be presented here with a light touch, I am very aware that finding your guidance was – and is – a personal and sometimes solitary journey, and I deeply respect you all for the ongoing courage it takes to recognise and to act upon inner knowing.

Special thanks to Elizabeth Papapetrou who helped me to complete the puzzle in the final week; to Nicky Leach who appeared at the perfect time to share the nuances of the writer's journey (and for strawberries *with* cream) and to James Twyman, "Emissary of Love," for permission to use an extract from one of Thomas's letters.

Thank you to my dear friend and brother, Greg Friedman, for consistent, grounding steadiness, wacky humour, and encouragement in the truest sense of the word. To Ann Harvey, Cynthia Fulreader, Lucy Loscocco, Narayani Stein, Wendy Feldman Bohoskey and Joanna Walter who have listened "behind my words" for many years: thank you for your deep wisdom and sister presence in my life. Many thanks to my twin-sister of birth, Sarah Newfeld Green, who has shared the journey with me from before the beginning, and continues to do so. To Bruce Scott, thank you for your gentle friendship, nudging me beyond the familiar, and letting me play with you in your own writing adventures. Thanks to Nura, Kathleen Loeks and Judy Scher, for not letting me stay small, and to Genoa Bliven for reminding me of the seriousness of what I came here to do – and *how* to enjoy it!

Respect and acknowledgment of the many women in the community of Northern New Mexico who are willing to stand up and be counted, especially Chellis Glendinning, Kathy Sanchez, and Consuelo Luz. Writing is a political act, and this is just the beginning. And to all women, children, teenagers, and men who stand up and are *not* counted, or who are told to sit back down. Stand up again! Know that your voice and your presence counts – and we are watching and listening.

To my beloved daughter, Mikhaila, one who stands up and wonders if she is heard. You are. Sit down only when writing your provocative and searing poetry. And, too, my dearest son, Joss, who ate an awful lot of barbecued chicken wings from the natural foods' deli as I sat at my computer. I'm thrilled that you learned that writing from the heart is as important as getting the facts straight. To my ex-husband, Diego Mulligan, thank you for being a true co-parent, and actually cooking *real* meals (I'll feed the kids while you're writing your book!).

I draw daily inspiration and spiritual sustenance from many traditions and teachers: From my east-European Jewish roots, from the poetry of Rumi and Hafiz, of Pablo Neruda, and Mary Oliver. From don Miguel Ruiz, Mata Amritanandamayi Devi (Ammachi), from the writers of the Buddhist dharma, from the solitude of silence, and the wild beauty of the natural world. I see the unity in so many paths and feel it mingle inside me.

And to the Source of all from where my own inner voice springs: I am listening, and remembering to give thanks.

Carly, October 2002

In Search of the Magic of Findhorn

by Karin Bogliolo & Carly Newfeld,

illustrated by Marko Pogacnik

242 pages paperback

published by Findhorn Press

isbn 1-899171-69-X

Many years ago, *The Magic of Findhorn*, a bestselling book, captured the imagination of the world and caused a multitude of people to visit the community and experience for themselves a new and exciting way of working and living together. Now, more than a quarter of a century later, both the Findhorn Community and the world have changed considerably and Karin Bogliolo, a former long-term community member, returns on a quest to see if the magic is still there. Encouraged by her innovative writer friend, Carly Newfeld, who lived at Findhorn in the early 70's, Karin begins to build a fascinating, fresh picture of the ground-breaking community as it is today.

Karin's quirky, down-to-earth personality and sense of humour enliven her investigations. She talks to present members, engages in their daily lives and challenges, shares their family meals, and recounts their differing viewpoints – all the while re-living her own experiences of Findhorn. Despite the difficulties caused by growth, finances, changing personalities and the departure and death of co-founder Peter Caddy, is there still magic at Findhorn? Do people ever leave–even when they go away?

If you have ever visited the Findhorn Community, whether for a day, a week, a month or for many years, this book will help you remember your experience and give you an insight into where the community is now–in the 21st century. For those of you who haven't yet visited the community, this book may be the one that finally tempts you to make the journey. At the very least it will transport you to a space deep inside yourself where you may just connect with magic.